Archaeology
at Santa Elena

Doorway to the Past

by

Stanley South

D0234240

THE UNIVERSITY OF SOUTH CAROLINA

SOUTH CAROLINA INSTITUTE OF ARCHAEOLOGY AND ANTHROPOLOGY

Popular Series 2

Columbia
1991

Table of Contents

Acknowledgements

This book describes numerous research projects carried out between 1979 and 1991 at Santa Elena on Parris Island through the auspices of the South Carolina Institute of Archaeology and Anthropology at the University of South Carolina. Funding was provided by the Institute, The National Geographic Society, *The National Geographic Magazine*, The National Science Foundation, The National Endowment for the Humanities, The Explorers Club of New York, The Robert L. Stephenson Archaeological Research Fund, The United States Marine Corps, the Spanish Government, and The Columbian Quincentennial Commission of South Carolina.

The Commission's Chairman, Chester B. DePratter, contributed personal funding and undertook a fund-raising project, making the 1991 expedition possible. Bruce Rippeteau, Director of the South Carolina Institute of Archaeology and Anthropology and State Archaeologist at the University of South Carolina also provided funding support from Institute operating funds. Thanks to Steve Wise at the Parris Island Museum for his support and cooperation. I am grateful to all these agencies and individuals for making our research at Santa Elena possible.

There is not space enough to acknowledge the valuable contribution made by my crew members and colleagues who have worked with me through the years on this enjoyable and challenging adventure. They have been acknowledged individually in the reports for each expedition. Some of them are shown at work in the illustrations herein. I especially thank those volunteers who worked so hard for the success of the 1991 project sponsored by the Quincentennial Commission. Without their contributions the project would not have been possible.

I enthusiastically acknowledge the United States Marine Corps who gave permission for me to excavate on the property under their jurisdiction and provided logistics help that made a major contribution to the projects.

I thank my colleagues, Chester DePratter and Albert C. Goodyear, who urged me to undertake this book for the public reader and made the funds available for its publication. I thank my colleague Edward Aylward of the Department of Spanish, Italian and Portuguese at the University of South Carolina for his help with coin nomenclature. I also thank my co-workers at the South Carolina Institute of Archaeology and Anthropology at the University of South Carolina for their many assistances during the preparation of this book. A special thanks to Carole Shealy who allowed me to use her laser printer to produce this book.

Special thanks go to my wife, Janet Ross Reddy, and to Chester DePratter for their excellent suggestions and for their editorial expertise in combing out many burrs from the text before publication.

I am indebted to the copyright holders, publishers, and owners of paintings who have allowed me to reproduce details to illustrate this book. These are: Abaris Books, Inc., New York; Sir Alfred Beit, London; The Art Institute of Chicago; The Catedral de Sevilla, Spain; The Florida Historical Society; The Historiches Museum, Dresden, Germany; The Kunsthistorisches Museum, Vienna; The Musée du Louvre, Paris; The Museo del Prado, Madrid, Spain; and the United States Marine Corps.

Preface

Chester B. DePratter, PhD
Chairman, Columbian Quincentennial Commission
of South Carolina

Between 1566 and 1587, the Spanish town of Santa Elena was the most northern of the several outposts established by Pedro Menéndez to defend Spanish Florida against encroachment by the French and English. For a brief period after it was first settled, Santa Elena served as Menéndez' capital, and its population ranged from a few dozen to several hundred over the next two decades. Bad relations with local Indians and Sir Francis Drake's sack of St. Augustine in 1586 led to the abandonment of Santa Elena in 1587.

For more than 300 years, Santa Elena was known only through historical accounts. Its exact location was lost. Then, in 1923, more than 300 years after the Spaniards abandoned this remote outpost, George H. Osterhout, a Major in the U.S. Marine Corps, conducted excavations within the outlines of a partially-filled moat on Parris Island, South Carolina. Major Osterhout found posts used in the construction of the fort, and he recovered many objects from the floor of the moat and from the remains of buildings within its confines. The Major, not a trained archaeologist, identified the objects he found as French, and he concluded that he had found French Charlesfort which was occupied from 1562 to 1563. A few years later, the United States Congress placed a monument within the fort, identifying it as Charlesfort. That monument is still there today.

Major Osterhout excavated only in a single fort, the outlines of which were still visible at the time of his work. Had he dug farther north along the bluffline, Major Osterhout would have found the remains of another fort and a sixteenth century town, and he would have known that it was not Charlesfort that he had discovered.

In the decades following Major Osterhout's excavations, debate raged among historians and archaeologists over whether he had truly found Charlesfort, or whether he had found the remains of one of Santa Elena's forts. In 1979, archaeologist Stanley South returned to the site where Major Osterhout had worked 66 years earlier, and he soon resolved the question. The site was Spanish Santa Elena.

From 1979 to 1985 and again in 1991, archaeologist South led research teams that excavated the remains of the town and forts of Santa Elena. He worked in Osterhout's fort and found that it was, in fact, the remains of Fort San Marcos, built by Spaniards between 1577 and 1587. North along the shoreline, South found another fort, Fort San Felipe, constructed betweens 1574 and 1576. And between the two forts, South found what remains of the town of Santa Elena. This volume describes the result of those excavations.

The Columbian Quincentennial Commission of South Carolina is extremely pleased to be part of Stanley South's continuing excavations at Santa Elena. His work provides us with an opportunity to bring before the public a little-known segment of South Carolina's history. With Mr. South's kind permission, we have opened up the excavations at Santa Elena to unlimited public visitation during April and May of 1991, 1992, and 1993 as the excavations proceed. We have also invited teachers from throughout the state to bring their classes to visit the site while excavations are underway, and we have hired guides and interpreters to provide each visitor with as much information as possible about South Carolina's Native American peoples and the early European settlements here.

This volume contains a brief overview of what has been learned so far through archaeology at Santa Elena. As excavations continue, we will learn more about the town layout with its plaza and streets, lined with houses of soldiers and settlers. We may be able to see the remains of the church, and perhaps there will be a cemetery nearby. We will learn much more about the daily lives of the people who lived here and about their interaction with the Native

Americans who occupied the nearby islands and mainland. Each year will reveal new and exciting discoveries at Santa Elena. My fellow commission members and I invite you to join us at Santa Elena as Mr. South digs deeper into South Carolina's early history.

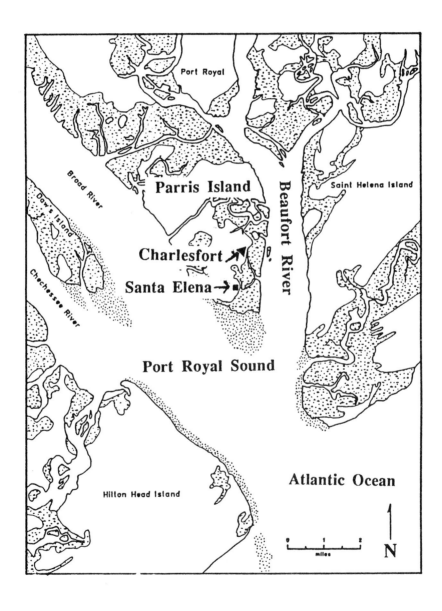

Chapter 1

A Spanish Colonial Overview

As time passes, we look back with ever-increasing
interest on the life and adventures of the earliest explorers and
settlers on this continent; and particularly so upon those of the
courageous men who came in the first century after Columbus.
Any traces of their forts and dwelling places, or any relics
rendered precious by their use, have for the most of us a
fascination powerful enough to even divert our attention from
present modern wonders such as the Airplane, the Radio,--and,
yes, also, even from the "Movies".   Major George H.
Osterhout, Jr., U.S.M.C. (*Marine Corps Gazette*, June, 1923).

Historical archaeology in America explores those places
where Europeans settled on Native American lands. Our knowledge
of what happened in those settlements has come mostly from the
documents recorded by these early explorers and settlers and we use
those accounts that have survived to write history.   Through
archaeological excavation, historical archaeology goes beyond those
fragments on which our history is based, to learn about the events,
the people, the things they used, and the places that history failed to
record. This book tells the story of the archaeology that has been
carried out on the site of Santa Elena, the capital of Spanish "La
Florida," now called Southeastern North America. Before the door
of archaeology was opened, however, I looked for a moment
through the window of history to put our archaeological work into
perspective.

To do this I used the published history of Santa Elena in
Jeannette T. Connor's *Colonial Records of Spanish Florida* and a
report by historian Paul Hoffman on the forts at Santa Elena,
prepared for the *The National Geographic Magazine*. Also valuable
was the article by Mary Ross on *The Spanish Settlement of Santa
Elena (Port Royal) in 1578*.   I also used *Santa Elena: A Brief
History of the Colony, 1566-1587* by Eugene Lyon, and his book

1

The Enterprise of Florida. Also useful was Gene Waddell's book *Indians of the South Carolina Lowcountry, 1562-1751.*

The sixteenth century was a time of exploration of the western hemisphere. In the early part of that century the Spaniards explored and exploited the Caribbean and parts of Central and South America. Cortez carried out the conquest of Mexico. Ponce de Leon, Lucas Vázquez de Ayllón, and Panfilo de Narváez attempted to colonize the new lands in North America.

Coastal South Carolina, Georgia, and Florida became the focus of Spain's exploration and colonization attempts following its incursions into Mexico, Peru, and the Caribbean. An early Spanish discovery of these lands came on June 24, 1521, when Pedro de Quexo and Francisco Gordillo sailed into Port Royal Sound near what is now Beaufort, South Carolina. The new land was called "A new Andalusia," by Lucas Vázquez de Ayllón, a backer of the expedition, along with Juan Ortiz de Matienzo and Diego Cavellero. Besides discovering land, the voyage captured and took back to Spain some sixty Native Americans who were lured aboard ship.

In 1526, following another voyage by Quexo, sponsored again by Ayllón, Ayllón himself led a colonizing expedition and established the first European settlement in the Southeast, thought to be south of Port Royal Sound, on the coast of present day Georgia. They called the colony San Miguel de Gualdape. Ayllón explored the large bay of Port Royal Sound on "St. Helena's Day" and named it Santa Elena. South Carolina was called the land of Chicora.

From 1539 to 1542, Hernando de Soto led an expedition of over 600 men into the interior of the Southeast, visiting the great chiefdom of Cofitachequi, located near what is now Camden, South Carolina. A goal of these expeditions to the interior was to search for the precious metals and pearls reported to be in these parts.

The DeSoto expedition was followed by the Tristan de Luna expedition, starting from Mobile Bay, with over 1000 strong, with the goal of establishing a town to be called Santa Elena. Only a part of this group eventually arrived by ship in Port Royal Sound in 1560. The town was not established at this time.

In the early 1560s, Spain and France clashed over control of the New World in the land the Spaniards called "La Florida." The French sought to establish a foothold through occupation, and built two forts in 1562 and 1564, the first French occupation in the Southeast. The first, called Charlesfort, built by Jean Ribault, was on Parris Island in Port Royal Sound, and the second, Fort Caroline, was built near the Saint John's River in Florida by Rene Laudonnière. Violence raged as the Spaniards responded to these incursions into lands they had discovered and explored.

In 1566, in response to the French occupations, Spanish Admiral Pedro Menéndez de Avilés established the Spanish settlement of Santa Elena on what is now Parris Island in South Carolina. It was to become the capital of Spanish *La Florida*, an area encompassing most of North America. Our interest is primarily in the area from the Chesapeake Bay to the southern tip of the present state of Florida. Spain built a number of defensive outposts, such as the one at St. Augustine, along the coast.

There were two Santa Elena settlements in the same location. The first dated from 1566 to 1576, when it was attacked and burned by Native Americans. A new Santa Elena was begun in 1577, and lasted until 1587, when it was abandoned after Sir Francis Drake burned St. Augustine. During this twenty-one year period, several hundred colonists, including women and children, farmers, merchants, lawyers, craftsmen, Indians and solders lived in the city and her forts.

During this time, three forts were constructed, each following the other, at Santa Elena. The first, called Fort San Salvador, was built on a low sandy bar in 1566, but it was soon damaged by fire. Fort San Felipe was built on higher ground in 1574, and was burned in an attack by Native Americans in the summer of 1576. The next year, a new fort, San Marcos, was built, using timbers brought from St. Augustine. There were a number of repairs and additions to this fort through the years, until it was dismantled in 1587.

By October, 1569, there were 327 colonists representing a variety of crafts and occupations in residence in the capital city. City government or *concejo*, had been empowered to issue land to its people following one of Spain's oldest institutions called "municipal liberties." Santa Elena was a thriving capital and port.

As early as the settlement of Santa Elena seems to us today, taking place more than one hundred years before the English arrived at Charles Towne (now Charleston), South Carolina in 1670, we can marvel at the vastness of the Spanish empire in the New World. In 1566, it contained over 160,000 Spaniards from Mexico to Peru, and throughout the Caribbean.

The settlement at Santa Elena took place almost two decades before Sir Walter Raleigh's "lost colony" of Roanoke (in North Carolina) became lost in 1585. A baby born at Santa Elena's founding would have been over forty years old when Virginia's Jamestown colony was first settled in 1609; that same individual would have been over half a century old before the Pilgrims landed at Plymouth, Massachusetts in 1620.

From Santa Elena, Spain's goals of conquest and settlement were taken into the interior and up the coast of the American continent by two different groups. In 1566 and 1568, Juan Pardo made important journeys from Santa Elena to the interior as far as the present state of Tennessee, in a search for mineral wealth. He established five tiny forts along the way, hoping to stand against a nation of Native Americans. In 1570, priests of the Jesuit order moved up the coast to the Chesapeake Bay area, in an attempt to bring Christianity to the Native Americans and establish a mission to win souls. The mission failed when the Spaniards were killed by Native Americans.

The city of Santa Elena was abandoned in 1587 at the order of the Spanish government after the British ships of Sir Francis Drake attacked and burned St. Augustine. Citizens moved to St. Augustine and Havana, Cuba. The Spaniards continued to maintain missions in the area of South Carolina and coastal Georgia through the seventeenth century.

By the time the English arrived with their "Port Royal Expedition" in 1670, the Spaniards had made several impacts on the native population of the Southeast. The great chiefdoms, such as the one at Cofitachequi, were reduced in population and declining by the time of the English arrival. Having contracted diseases brought by the Spaniards, the large Native American population throughout the region had been drastically reduced in the first 150 years of the Spanish presence. Many groups had accepted a version of Christianity brought by the Spaniards, and the men had given up their traditional plural wives and other ritual customs. Material tribute was paid by Native Americans to Santa Elena, and after that town was abandoned, to St. Augustine. The last major effort at resistance to the European invasion in this area by Native Americans came with the Yamassee War with the English in 1715.

In the late seventeenth century the arrival of the English brought conflict with the Spaniards, with attacks and threat of attack constantly present between the competing European powers struggling for control of Spanish Florida. By 1763, a declining Spanish power base and aggresssive English harassment tipped control to the English. The Spanish presence in Florida, however, was a significant political and economic factor in the colonization of North America in the eighteenth century.

As a result of pressure from the English in South Carolina, Florida came under English rule in 1763 and remained in English control until 1783, when it again came under Spanish rule. In 1821, Florida became an American territory, ending the Spanish colonial era in the Southeast.

America's Spanish colonial heritage will be of increasing importance in the decades to come as the Spanish-speaking population increases. Much interest will be generated also by the 500th anniversary of the voyages of Columbus. Our research is helping to lay the groundwork for this quincentennial, toward a greater understanding of the interaction between Native Americans and Spaniards during the neglected century of the Spanish colonial period.

6

French ships of Jean Ribault exploring Port Royal Sound at Parris Island in 1562. (De Bry engraving of Le Moyne watercolor. De Bry Plate 5. Photo courtesy of the U.S. Marine Corps.)

Chapter 2

The Search for Santa Elena Begins

> The history of the Carolinas opens with a dramatic
> Spanish chapter. It is a long one with many episodes, each
> vibrant with colorful action. Outstanding in this full-laden
> chronicle is the story of Santa Elena, a romantic tale of human
> drama staged on Carolina's soil. Mary Ross, historian. (The
> Georgia Historical Quarterly, 1925).

In 1978, Joseph Judge, Associate Editor of *The National Geographic Magazine*, became interested in locating Santa Elena, the capital of Spanish *La Florida* , thought to be on Parris Island, South Carolina. Judge contacted Robert L. Stephenson, Director of the Institute of Archaeology and Anthropology at the University of South Carolina, where I work as an historical archaeologist specializing in excavating colonial sites. Judge was also interested in identifying a fort on Parris Island, South Carolina, dug into by a Marine Corps major in 1923.

Judge also contacted Charles Fairbanks and Kathleen Deagan, archaeologists involved with the excavation of St. Augustine and other Spanish colonial sites, and historians Eugene Lyon and Paul Hoffman, experts on the Spanish colonial era. He wanted to hold a meeting on Parris Island on the presumed site of Spanish Fort San Marcos, to discuss the possibility of doing archaeology to explore the Spanish past.

Later in 1978, a meeting was arranged and several of this group met on Parris Island on a fort site partially excavated by Marine Corps Major George H. Osterhout in 1923. The purpose was to introduce us to the site and to select a likely place for archaeology to be conducted to determine who had built the fort. The site covers an area several hundred yards square along the shore of the Beaufort River and beneath the Parris Island Marine Corps

7

Golf Course. This meeting marked the first time I had stood on the site the major had identified as French Charlesfort, but which we believed to be the site of the Spanish Fort San Marcos, the last fort guarding Santa Elena. There we saw a monument erected by the United States Congress in 1925, recognizing Charlesfort built by Jean Ribault. We also saw concrete pillars marking the outline of the fort the major had excavated.

Concrete pillars marking the location of the northwest bastion and the west side of the fort found by Major Osterhout in 1923. (Photo No. 12, August 1, 1936, courtesy of the U.S. Marine Corps.)

All agreed that the Parris Island site was of major interest with potential for revealing much about who was there in the past and what they left behind. Major Osterhout's identification of the site as French Charlesfort of 1562 had caused a controversy in the 1920s with some historians identifying the site as that of Spanish Fort San Marcos at Santa Elena. We shared this latter position.

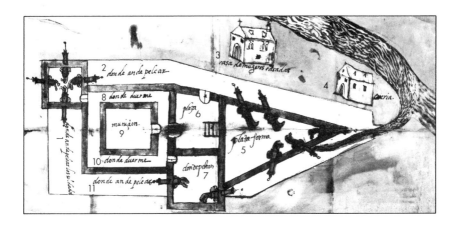

The map of Fort San Marcos used to locate the site of Fort San Felipe. The northwest bastion showing four guns is seen in the upper left corner. The gun pointing toward the top of the page pointed toward the burned ruin of Fort San Felipe. (From Archivo General de Indias, Seville. Mapas y Planos, Mexico 46. From Hoffman 1978, Fig. 8.)

We had with us a copy of a map of Fort San Marcos, and a document of 1578, stating that the north gun of the northwest bastion shown on the map pointed to the site of the previous fort, San Felipe, burned in a Native American attack in 1576.

Our thinking was that if the northwest bastion of Major Osterhout's fort was indeed the northwest bastion shown on the Fort San Marcos map, we should be able to look toward the north from that marked bastion toward the site of Fort San Felipe. We thought the fort would have been close to the water, with Santa Elena behind it. What we saw when we looked north from that bastion was the edge of the high ground and the marsh beside the Beaufort River. From this we concluded that some of the high ground had been washed away. The remaining high ground was of great interest to us. Would it be the site of the town and fort? How much had been washed away by storms?

As we speculated on what we might find if we dug on the high ground in the woods beside the golf course, the area indicated by the clue from the map, I looked down, and there at our feet lay a musketball, an Indian pottery fragment, and a piece of Spanish majolica, the type of tin-ash glazed pottery we knew we should find on a sixteenth century Spanish colonial site! To me these fragments represented a major archaeological doorway to the past.

These material links to the Spanish colonial past were more real than words written on a page. These clues were the kind of evidence we would need if we were to solve the mystery of who built the fort on which we stood. The potsherd was not French! It was a glazed majolica fragment of a bowl of a type known as Columbia Plain. We knew from research that it was made in Spain in the sixteenth century. We had found our first archaeological clues to Santa Elena's past beneath our feet!

Joe Judge's gathering of colleagues interested in the Spanish colonial past resulted in the decisions that I would pursue archaeology on the site and request funding from the National Geographic Society.

As my companions walked away from the fort toward the north to look for a likely place to look for the ruins of Santa Elena, I leaned against one of the concrete markers Major Osterhout used to mark the fort he found. A melancholy mood mixed with anticipation of the archaeological challenge lying ahead swept over me. I felt that I was standing on the threshold of a doorway to the past.

A Columbia Plain majolica bowl from Santa Elena.

Chapter 3

The Sampling Project Begins

In 1979, I received a small grant from the University of South Carolina to carry out a one week expedition on the site. Our first goal at the site we suspected of being Santa Elena was to locate evidence that it was either Spanish colonial Santa Elena of 1566-1587, or French Charlesfort of 1562. To identify Santa Elena we needed to find additional sixteenth century Spanish artifacts such as the one sherd of majolica we had found on the fort on our first visit to the site. Through such pottery we could date the site and identify the nationality of the people who lived there.

Besides artifacts, through which we would identify the people who onced lived on the site and something of their way of life, we needed to find evidence of their houses. We knew that Spanish colonial buildings of this period were built of wooden posts and clay-daubed walls baked hard when the houses burned. We would be searching for such baked clay daub, not brick and stone or a much later material called tabby. We were also interested in finding evidence of the Native Americans they dealt with in their daily lives.

Although archaeology has its romantic moments, it is a process that requires the discipline and rigor of science to achieve its goals. It would be ideal if archaeologists could dig an entire site to recover all the possible information buried within the soil, but this can seldom be afforded in terms of time and funding. Therefore, almost all archaeology is a process of taking a sample of the information a site has to offer and interpreting from the sample something of the broader picture represented by the bits and pieces recovered. Computers are used in this process.

I knew from the documentation that the first city of Santa Elena was burned by the Native American attack on the city in 1576. Further, that the second Santa Elena was abandoned and the remaining houses burned by the Spaniards in 1587. This was done

11

after British privateer, Sir Francis Drake, attacked and burned St. Augustine. The burned ruins of Santa Elena houses in the form of charred posts might still be in the ground because charcoal does not decay with time.

More importantly for our sampling project, I knew from documentary research that the houses likely were built of clay plastered over a wattling of vines and sticks, with roofs thatched with palmetto leaves. If this information were correct, I also knew that when such a house burned, the heat would bake parts of the clay wall into hard brick-like fragments that would survive hundreds of years in the earth. This material, called fired clay daub, still would remain in the vicinity of where each house once stood. I knew, too, that some of the houses in the second Santa Elena had their clay walls and roofs coated with lime plaster made of oystershells. The location of daub and plaster concentrations from houses was the major goal of our sampling plan.

Because we could not excavate the entire area we thought contained the remains of Santa Elena we used a sampling design to allow us to get a general idea of where houses might have been located by trying to pinpoint the concentrations of fired clay daub. Our theory was that if we could dig sample holes in the area in the woods between the golf course which now occupied the site and the edge of the high ground at the marsh, we just might hit on some concentrations of fired clay daub remaining from burned Spanish colonial houses. Where no house had stood, there would be no daub. These data could then manipulated in what is called a SYMAP computer program that produces a map of the concentrations.

The random hole pattern we used to search for Santa Elena is known scientifically as a "stratified systematic unaligned subsurface sampling design," but we refer to it simply as the sampling design. Our idea was to dig three-foot square holes in a controlled manner over an area 90 by 420 feet in size, one hole for each 30-foot square area. One three-foot square is one percent of a 30-foot area. This one percent sampling of the 90 by 420 foot area would require us to dig 42 squares in one week to recover the data necessary for our computer drawn map of daub and pottery concentrations.

To pick where to put the first 90 by 420 foot research sample frame, I walked to a relatively cleared area beneath the live oak trees where our work would be shaded from the sun while we were digging, and drove an iron rod into the ground to serve as a starting point for my mapping. I then laid out the area using a surveying transit. The research frame had to be located between the fairway of the adjacent golf course and the edge of the marsh. Once our 90 by 420 foot research frame was laid out on the ground, we chose the location of each three-foot square by using a table of random numbers to select the position each square. With the location of each square designated by numbered flagging pins, my family and other volunteers began excavating our first holes into the site.

Another idea I had was that broken Spanish pottery fragments would be found around each house in greater density than away from the houses, since experience from past excavations on British colonial sites had shown that people during the colonial period tended to discard trash close to their houses. This is one of the ideas we were interested in testing. We wanted to see if the Spanish colonists also discarded trash directly around their dwellings as the British did much later. As our search progressed, we found that they did.

Michael Hartley in one of the sample holes used to locate the town of Santa Elena and Fort San Felipe. The power screen sifter in the background is used to separate artifacts from dirt.

14

Our method of excavating the three-foot squares involved removal of the dark humic topsoil with shovels to the level of the undisturbed subsoil, and screening the soil through power sifters with a one-quarter inch mesh hardware cloth. All recovered objects were placed in appropriately numbered bags to be washed and analyzed later. Daub would be weighed and pottery sherds counted and programmed into a computer to produce a map showing where they concentrated. There we would dig to see if a house could be found.

From the first square we dug, it became apparent that we were excavating a sixteenth century Spanish colonial site. We found Spanish made Columbia Plain majolica and fragments of large Spanish olive jars, pottery types known to date from the sixteenth century. Native American pottery of the sixteenth century was also present in considerable quantity, testifying to the interaction of the Spanish colonists with local Native Americans. We were greatly encouraged as each hole was excavated to the subsoil level, and we found pottery and fired clay daub as anticipated.

A Spanish olive jar from a well in Fort San Felipe.

We soon learned that in some of the squares the plowed topsoil zone, which we designated as level A, had beneath it a relatively undisturbed, dark soil zone which we called level B. This darker zone was about two to three inches thick and contained Spanish artifacts, daub, bone, and Indian pottery in greater numbers than the overlying topsoil. The B level appeared to be an original Spanish period soil zone that was sometimes compacted, as though it had once been a heavily packed, hardened surface, such as would result from a house floor being baked as the house burned. This evidence for possible house floors was of great interest to us as we examined the sample squares. By the end of the first day of work, with Spanish and Indian pottery seen in all squares, and the presence of quantities of fired clay daub and iron spikes and postholes in others, we were convinced that we had discovered a Spanish site and not French Charlesfort. Our sampling project was abundantly fulfilling our expectations, but a greater surprise awaited us a few days later when about half the 42 squares had been dug.

A fragment of a Native American pot from Fort San Felipe.

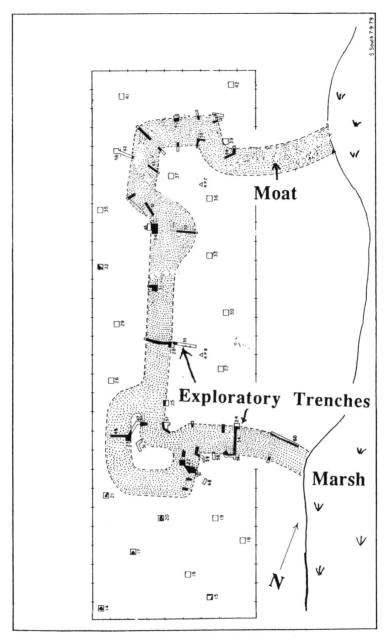

The outline of the moat of Fort San Felipe drawn by connecting the ditch edges discovered in squares and exploratory trenches in the first sample frame . Half of the fort had been lost to erosion at the edge of the site.

Chapter 4

Fort San Felipe Is Found

When we finished removing the Level B soil from the bottoms of the squares we could see postholes in some cases, ditches in others, as well as oystershell filled pits containing Spanish objects. These features contained soil darker than the subsoil sand around them. In some of the squares we found the discolored soil and straight edges characteristic of a filled-in ditch. After several of these stains had been found, we noticed that some of the edges lined up. It became apparent that we had discovered a ditch of some sort. The next question we asked was how wide this ditch might be, since we had not seen both sides of it in any square. To answer this question we cut a long exploratory trench to the subsoil level to attempt to determine the width of the ditch.

We soon noticed that there appeared to be two ditches aligned at right angles to each other. We cut the exploratory trench only slightly wider than our shovels, carefully cleaning the bottom periodically to see if the dark soil of the ditch continued and trying to find the lighter soil we expected to find on the other side of the ditch. Both ditches proved to be sixteen feet wide. This told us that we were definitely not dealing with a drain from a house, but some far wider ditch. Such a ditch, sixteen feet wide, is more characteristic of a fortification ditch than a domestic household. Had we found a fort moat?

After much discussion we decided to continue to dig more exploratory trenches under the assumption that we likely had found the moat of Fort San Felipe, to which the gun on the Fort San Marcos map had pointed. I suspended our search for daub and pottery in the sample squares to concentrate on the new discovery. I was excited by the possibility of learning how large Fort San Felipe was, and was anxious to determine its shape. By digging trenches and connecting the area between the points on the edge of the ditch, much like a dot-to-dot game, I was able to determine that a

18

two bastioned fort moat lay beneath my feet at this area of our research frame. While searching for clues to the city of Santa Elena I had found the half of the moat of Fort San Felipe, dug in 1574, that had not eroded away.

The discovery of this Spanish fort verified our assumption that the fort Major Osterhout had identified as Charlesfort was actually Spanish Fort San Marcos. We held a press conference at the National Geographic Society headquarters in Washington, D.C. to announce our discovery. It was big news, as the front page of the *New York Times* for July 13, 1979, reported. Now we had the ruins of two Spanish colonial forts that documentation indicated were located at Santa Elena, verifying our belief that we were dealing with that city. Our effort now turned back toward our search for evidence of houses in the town of Santa Elena through our sample squares.

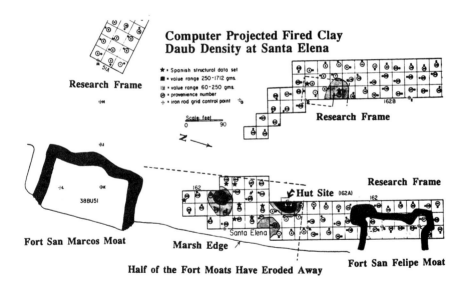

The outlines of the remaining halves of the moats of Forts San Marcos and San Felipe. The computer-drawn dark spots between them indicate concentrations of fired clay daub from burned houses in the town of Santa Elena, suggesting that the town lay between the two fort locations. The location of three sample square research frames used in our search for daub and pottery concentrations is shown.

Chapter 5

The Sampling Project Concludes

The discovery of the moat of Fort San Felipe in the bottom of some of our sample holes detracted us for awhile from our goal of locating house ruins in Santa Elena. We were half-way through our week's project and still had many holes to dig to get data for a computer print-out of daub and Spanish pottery density. To us, a burned daub concentration means a burned house and a concentration of Spanish pottery with it means a burned Spanish house.

As we continued to dig our sample squares, people came to see the fort they had heard about in the news and on television. At this time the fort was not something that anyone could see who visited the site. I had to explain that it existed beneath a blanket of soil, and that our sample holes and exploratory trenches, like small windows, had revealed enough points along the edge of the moat so that a dot-to-dot map of the moat outline could be seen on paper. I showed them the map I had drawn from the slot trenches and squares we had dug to help them understand what we had found (p. 16).

Many looked at me strangely, as though I had invented the fort because what I showed them was so foreign to their concept of what a ruin should look like. "Where are the cut stones like we saw at Castillo de San Marcos at St. Augustine?" some asked. I had to reply that that fort was one hundred years more recent than Fort San Felipe and had been built in a totally different manner using large quarried stone blocks. Clues to Fort San Felipe and Santa Elena were far more difficult to discover and to interpret because the evidence was in the form of soil discolorations in the earth.

Visitors also wanted to see Santa Elena and all I could show them was a grassy area beneath live oak trees and say that I was confident, based on our sampling, that the ruins of the houses of Santa Elena lay somewhere beneath that carpet of grass.

19

When the last of the 42 three-foot square holes was dug, I returned to the University of South Carolina to weigh the daub and count the pottery fragments and to run the computer maps showing the density of artifacts within our 90 by 420 foot research frame. The house search continued there as the data we had recovered were fed into the computer to produce the map of daub and pottery density we had designed the project to produce.

The maps the computer drew for us were exciting in that they allowed us to determine which artifacts clustered together. Two maps showed a concentration of fired clay daub and sixteenth century Spanish pottery at the southwest corner of our research frame. This association strongly suggested that we would find a burned Spanish house ruin if we were to dig there. This is what we had been looking for because, to us, daub equals a house, and Spanish pottery associated with it equals a Spanish house, and a Spanish house ruin would mean we had found a Santa Elena ruin.

The computer-drawn maps, therefore, were as exciting as any discovery we had made in the field. They were the goal of our sampling project. Although we had found a few postholes in some squares, much larger areas needed to be dug before we could interpret them in relation to a structure. The small University of South Carolina grant had produced dramatic and rewarding results. We had a suspected Spanish house site from our computer map and a moat of Fort San Felipe to show for our one-week effort.

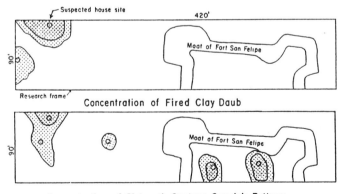

Concentration of Fired Clay Daub

Concentration of Sixteenth Century Spanish Pottery

Concentration of fired clay daub and Spanish pottery in the research frame that led to the discovery of a Santa Elena hut ruin.

Chapter 6

A Hut Ruin Is Discovered

The suspected house site was at the southwest corner of the research frame, 150 feet from the fort moat we had found. It was where Spanish pottery and fired clay daub were clustered. In the fall of 1979, I applied for funding to the National Geographic Society to excavate a 20 by 30 foot area around the daub and pottery cluster to test the assumption that a Spanish house would be found there. The funds were granted, and I soon began removing the topsoil blanket.

My goal was to discover a posthole pattern revealing the shape of the building, its size, the materials used in its construction and something of its function. Besides the architectural details, I was interested in learning, from the artifacts, something about the people who lived in the house and, from the food remains, something of their diet and daily activities relating to it.

As each five foot square was excavated, great care was taken as we reached the B zone beneath the topsoil zone. We had found that this level was likely a relatively undisturbed Spanish occupation surface. We soon began finding piles of fired clay daub beside postholes containing burned wooden posts that we later determined were yellow pine. When the entire 20 by 30 foot area was exposed, we had revealed a D-shaped pattern of nine postholes containing charcoal and fired clay daub. Daub piles from walls of a building had been created by the burning of the posts. Some burned posts were still in place in the postholes. The evidence indicated that a hut about twelve feet across, much like a Native American house, once stood where we had dug. Our sample plan had correctly predicted the location of a ruined structure. The Spanish pottery found with it suggested it dated from the Spanish occupation of the site.

Near the center of the twelve foot wide D-shaped hut ruin area, a scorched soil stain was found. This suggested that a central hearth had been located there, such as those found in the ruins of Native American houses. In such houses, the smoke rises and goes out a smokehole. It is likely that its roof was made of a flammable material such as palmetto thatch. If this was a Santa Elena house, it is interesting that it was made in the Native American manner. Perhaps the house burned in the Native American attack on Santa Elena in 1576.

The D-shaped circle of dark postholes at the hut ruin. I am examining the scorched hearth area. The strings outline the area of the hut and the postholes.

Beside one of the postholes, in a mass of fired clay wall-daub, charred corncobs with the kernels still on the cob were found that were probably hanging on the post at the time the structure burned. This corn was of particular interest in that it had twelve rows, a type characteristic of Mexican corn as opposed to Indian corn locally grown in the Santa Elena area, which usually had only eight rows. A 1568 document reported that a shipload of corn from Yucatan had arrived at Santa Elena. Perhaps we had found some of that corn.

A burned ear of Mexican corn found beside a post in the hut ruin.

From the size of the charred posts we learned that a sturdy structure was involved. From the impressions of Spanish moss and cane or cornstalks in the fired clay daub, we learned something of the wattling used in the construction of the building.

From the small size of this ruin and the fact that no porcelain or other high-status Spanish pottery was found in it, I interpreted its resident to be a servant or soldier, many of whom were quartered in the town rather than in the fort. The quantity of musketballs found in the house might also suggest that a soldier lived there because soldiers had access to weapons. Was this Native American style structure typical of Santa Elena or was it, as we suggested, a shelter for an individual with few resources, such as a servant, a soldier, or a slave? To answer this question we would have to discover and dig more ruins.

An interesting discovery at the hut site was that after the hut was in ruins, a vineyard had been planted over the site where the hut had stood. Parallel ditches were dug across the ruin in a typical manner of planting vineyards. Although this vineyard had nothing to do with the hut, having been planted long after it was in ruins, there were vineyards in Santa Elena when the hut stood. Father Rogel, who visited Santa Elena in 1568, reported a thriving vineyard there. Probably the grapes were used to make wine.

The corn, represented by the burned corn-on-the-cob, and bones of fish and animals recovered from the household trash deposit, are clues to the diet of the Santa Elena resident living in the hut. These include deer, pig and chicken, as well as all manner of seafood: oysters, mussels, conch, shark, catfish, sheepshead, sea trout, croaker, red and black drum fish and mullet. It is apparent that locally obtained seafood was an important part of the Santa Elena diet. Also from features around the hut we recovered samples of seeds that are revealing of the diet at Santa Elena. Recovered plant remains include sugar cane, hickory nuts, acorns, and maypop.

Also in the household trash deposit around the hut were pottery fragments from Spain and Italy, and Aztec Indian pottery from Mexico (p. 65). Only one fragment of Chinese Ming porcelain was found at the hut site, whereas much more was to be discovered later near larger homes.

From our excavation of the hut site we demonstrated the validity of our sampling approach for predicting the location of Santa Elena house ruins and we learned what one type of building in Santa Elena looked like. We also learned about the foods the people living there ate, and we recovered objects reflecting Santa Elena's connection with the world trade network so important to sixteenth century Spanish colonial life. The National Geographic Society grant had allowed us to discover information not known from historical documents alone.

An interpretive drawing of the D-shaped hut based on postholes and other architectural data recovered during excavation of the hut ruin. (Drawing by Darby Erd.)

Chapter 7

Santa Elena Is Found

The hut project in the fall of 1979 also involved extending the original sample frame toward the south. The success of my previous research sampling design in locating the hut site prompted me to continue the same approach as a discovery tool to try to reveal other house ruins in Santa Elena. Other research frames were dug. Through excavation of these research frames, composed of hundreds of three-foot squares, we learned where the heaviest concentration of Spanish colonial daub was located (p. 18).

Most important were those sample squares where additional architectural clues such as postholes, iron spikes, a hard-packed clay surface, and Spanish pottery were found (p. 13). Between Fort San Marcos and Fort San Felipe we saw a concentration of architecture-rich squares. Apparently, Fort San Felipe had stood at the northern edge of Santa Elena, and Fort San Marcos was built near the southern edge of the major cluster of houses in the city (p.18).

One of our sample squares south of the hut site had revealed a posthole and other diagnostic architectural characteristics. In order to discover whether this posthole was from a house, I cut a series of trenches north and south from that posthole and found other postholes in alignment with it. This posthole pattern seemed to represent the remains of an 18 by 20 foot structure. The second house from Santa Elena had been found.

One of the trenches I opened in searching for this house revealed a large hole measuring eight feet across. Because of the flecks of white sand in the fill soil of this hole, we suspected that it was very deep compared to the postholes, which contained no sand of this color. Recognition of soil colors reflecting past behavioral activity is known as "reading the dirt," which archaeologists do as routinely as reading the pages of books and manuscripts to obtain information contained there. Through experience at reading such soil clues, I predicted that this large hole, called by archaeologists a "feature," was a well, probably to supply water for the house adjacent to it. I was eager to dig a Spanish colonial well, but I knew I would have to return later to excavate this large feature. A proposal for funding would have to be written.

"Reading the dirt" beneath the Parris Island Golf Course to understand the postholes, ditches and midden-filled daub-processing pits of Santa Elena. Can you find the three processing pits? Two have been crossed by a vineyard ditch. The archaeologists are marking the edges of the features for mapping.

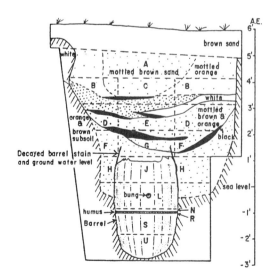

The Santa Elena barrel and drawing.

With the discovery of this second structural ruin and a possible well, I felt even more confident that I had found the site of Santa Elena. In 1981, I returned with another National Geographic Society grant to excavate the large feature and it indeed proved to be a Spanish colonial well. At the bottom of the hole sat a wooden barrel, with both ends removed, placed there by the Spaniards as a casing for the well. Because it was below the water table, the barrel had been preserved intact, complete with cork in the bung hole, and wooden and iron bands bound with woven basketry withes. To excavate below the water table, we installed well-points attached to pumps, allowing us to dig around the barrel and remove it from the earth where it had remained untouched for over four hundred years. Preserved in the barrel were seeds, leaves and other plant remains seldom seen by the archaeologist.

The profile of the well revealed that two barrels had been placed one above the other as a casing or liner for the well. The top barrel had been removed, probably to be used in a new well.

With the barrel removed from the well I turned again to the search for Santa Elena's houses. Several of my sample squares had revealed architectural data suggesting houses might be located there. I used this information to position an L-shaped area 30 by 100 feet in size, to look for posthole patterns where houses once stood.

The L-shaped area in which three Santa Elena house ruins were discovered. The archaeologist's grid corners form a pattern in the excavated area.

However, our search for postholes was not simple, for as we removed the topsoil blanket covering the Spanish occupation, we found layers of oystershell. From the Spanish objects among the shell, we knew we were looking at Spanish midden, the term used by archaeologists to describe trash and garbage, which, in this case, might have been thrown from Spanish houses. We had to clean off the shell layers to map and photograph their location before we could remove them to try to discover postholes from house ruins beneath the shell.

Jeanne Metropol using water to reveal midden layers of oystershells discarded from Spanish houses now lying beneath the Parris Island Golf Course.

As we removed these shells to look for postholes beneath, we found that the shell layers covered pits filled with more oystershells and other Spanish colonial midden. As we removed the contents of these pits we began to notice that several had gray clay-lined bottoms. Why would the Spaniards have dug clay in the marsh, where it is still to be seen today, and put it into pits they had dug? We knew that clay for daub walls had to be dug in the marsh. Perhaps, I deduced, the clay-lined pits had something to do with mixing daub for walls of buildings. We observed these pits carefully as we excavated them and removed the artifacts to try to answer this question.

With a number of these midden-filled, clay-lined features excavated, I interpreted them as pits used by the Spaniards to mix water, Spanish moss and sand to form daub for building house walls. These are the ingredients we could see in the burned daub we found. When the walls of a structure were completed, the yard would be full of these daub-processing pits. They then served as convenient garbage disposal holes for ashes from hearth fires, broken pottery, eggshells, and broken, damaged or unusable iron spikes and nails, musketballs, crossbow parts, and personal and religious ornaments, as well as pins, thimbles and other Spanish colonial things.

A partly excavated daub-processing pit in the L-shaped area. A Spanish majolica bowl fragment can be seen lying among oystershell midden in the pit.

Because the daub-processing pits were loaded with Spanish objects, we carefully dug them with a trowel so as to not damage anything. They were fun to dig because we never knew what we would find next. One of the interesting objects recovered was a cockspur from a rooster. If this rooster had fought for the Spaniards, he would be the earliest known fighting gamecock in South Carolina, good news to the athletic teams at the University of South Carolina represented by the gamecock.

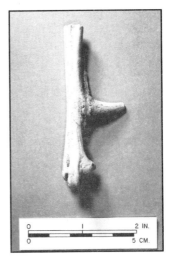

A cockspur from a garbage pit.

31

One bowl recovered from one of the garbage filled pits had a blue painted bird called a *partalot* painted on it. This bird is still used by Spanish potters today as a decorative motif on bowls and plates, and was used for hundreds of years before Santa Elena was occupied. We think most of the majolica found in Santa Elena was made in Seville, Spain. Many artifacts found in the layers and midden-filled features will be described in chapter 14.

Once colonists filled daub-processing pits with trash, such as broken majolica plates and bowls, and garbage from meals, such as chicken bones and oystershells, the colonists continued, out of habit, to throw things onto the area above the pits. This caused the layers of midden we saw. With the puzzle of the shell midden layers and the daub-processing pits understood to our satisfaction, I turned our attention again to the search for the postholes for houses, which we began to see as we removed the shell midden from the area.

Beneath the oystershell midden in the L-shaped area, we found posthole patterns of three of the houses, measuring 26, 32, and 42 feet in length respectively, with a width of 11 to 12 feet. They were around what appeared to be a courtyard about 44 by 51 feet in size. We had finally discovered the Santa Elena house postholes, which was the major goal of our 1981 project.

A posthole filled with oystershells.

By comparing the size of the rectangular posthole patterns of the Santa Elena houses with drawings of sixteenth century Spanish houses by Albert Manucy in his study of Hispanic folk architecture, I had a good idea of what a house in Santa Elena looked like.

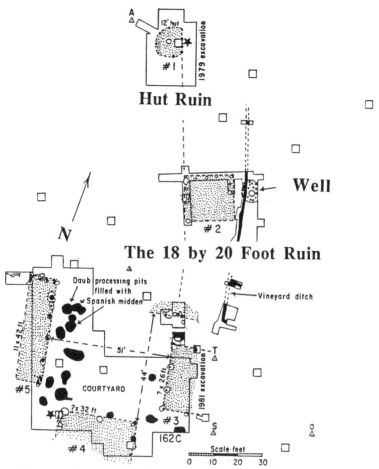

Hut Ruin

Well

The 18 by 20 Foot Ruin

Three House Ruins Around a Courtyard

A drawing showing the location of five structures in Santa Elena.

From the postholes, the daub, and the documents we were able to draw a sketch of the appearance of a Santa Elena house. This house is similar to those in the rural countryside of sixteenth century Spain.

Our excavations also recovered a few artifacts from the seventeenth century, the early eighteenth century, and the plantation period of the mid-nineteenth century. These were found in the topsoil above the Spanish occupation zone and occasionally in pits and ditches. These items were not our primary concern, but we methodically recorded their presence and treated all artifacts, regardless of their period of origin, as archaeological data capable of contributing to our understanding of the history of the site. Discoveries from the nineteenth century plantation period are discussed in Chapter 16.

That history also left archaeological remains from the use of the site by the United States Marine Corps. As we searched for evidence of Spanish structures, we found a number of sharply defined square and rectangular holes, some holding rotten posts. Whenever we saw these holes we noticed they cut into the Spanish features. The holes were in rows enclosing areas 10 by 50, 20 by 50, and 30 by 50 feet in size. Correlating these with a June, 1918 map, we determined that they were the remains of Marine Corps barracks. Rows of small rectangular wooden stake holes, measuring one by three inches, were also found. These we identified as holes for stakes used to pitch tents. These recent features revealed that a Marine Corps encampment with barracks and tents once stood on the site.

The artifacts found in the footing holes date from the period of World War I. Coins (pennies, dimes and quarters) dating from 1908 to 1919 helped us to date these rows of holes. Also found in the area of the posthole rows were U.S. Marine Corps buttons, a fork, and other military items marked "U.S.M.C.."

Even the activity on the Parris Island Marine Corps Golf Course was revealed in our L-shaped area, in the form of golf ball skins, shucked by the lawnmower blades, and wooden tees. Severe slices by less than proficient golfers sent golf balls whizzing past our heads on several occasions We now take provisions against possible injury, through permission of golf pro Mike DiPasquale, by moving the tee-off markers down the fairway well beyond our excavation area.

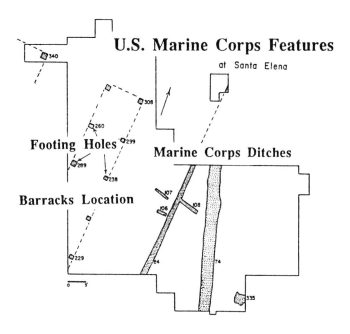

U.S. Marine Corps Features

at Santa Elena

Footing Holes

Barracks Location

Marine Corps Ditches

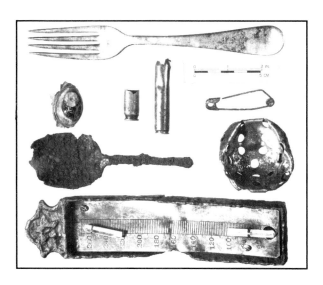

U.S. Marine Corps features and artifacts from the period of the First World War found in the L-shaped excavation area. Objects shown are: a nickle silver fork marked "U.S.M.C," a lightbulb base, two brass cartridge cases, a safety pin, an iron spoon, a strainer for a sink drain, and a cast iron thermometer for steam.

Chapter 8

Exploring Fort San Marcos

When I found the hut in 1979 I also wanted to do some archaeological sampling in the area of the walls of Fort San Marcos. I knew from the documents and maps that Fort San Marcos was a two story building, and I knew its shape before and after new additions were made. I knew that posts and lumber were brought from St. Augustine to build it. I knew that if the walls were plastered it might be with oystershell lime mortar. From Major Osterhout's digging I knew that the posts were made of cedar. From records of a 1578 inspection, I knew many details of the appearance and function of this fort built in 1577 by Pedro Menéndez Marqués.

A question I was interested in addressing was how much damage had been done to the remains of Fort San Marcos by hurricanes and the digging of Major George Osterhout, Jr. in 1923. Photographs he took revealed piles of dirt, posts taken from the fort wall, and pottery fragments. It was impossible to determine how much he had dug and how many posts he had removed from the fort wall, since no drawings or description of his work were available to us.

Part of my plan for the National Geographic Society sampling project at Fort San Marcos was to find surviving parts of walls on each of the sides of the fort outlined by concrete markers (p. 8). I would do this by digging a five foot square above the spot where I thought the walls would be located. These exploratory excavations revealed red cedar posts still in place on two sides of the fort. On the south wall we found one of the posts lying on its side in the ditch that once held it, and beside it was a wooden stake with white lead-base paint still covering it. This was one of the stakes Major Osterhout used to hold the string so that his trenches would have a proper military and archaeological neatness. I also found his

35

trench, which was very neat and straight, indicating the care with which he had dug. Our discovery of the orderly manner with which he dug convinced us that his work left much of Fort San Marcos still to be discovered in future excavations.

The cedar posts of Fort San Marcos were placed about eighteen inches apart, revealing that they were not part of a palisade wall, but likely were supporting posts for a board wall. Our excavations also revealed fragments of oystershell lime plaster that had fallen from the walls when the fort was burned. These fragments were plastered smooth on one side and showed the impression of boards on the other, revealing they had likely been plastered against a horizontally laid board wall nailed to the upright posts we found.

The dark outline of a ditch holding the west wall of Fort San Marcos, dug by Spaniards in 1577, seen in the bottom of a five foot test square, containing the bottom ends of two cedar posts still in place. The posts were brought from St. Augustine, along with the other lumber for use in building Fort San Marcos. They have survived for 400 years because they have been below the water table where oxygen could not cause them to rot.

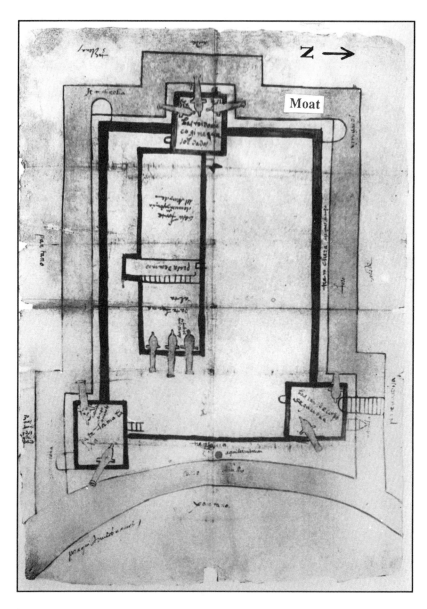

The map of Fort San Marcos after additions were made . (From Archivo General de Indias, Seville. Mapas y Planos, Florida y Luisiana 2. From Hoffman 1978, Fig. 9.) The bottom half of the fort has washed away. Visitors enter the fort site today by a bridge over the moat and across the bastion at the top.

Documents written during an inspection of Fort San Marcos say that its posts had rotted off at the ground and its triangular artillery platform would have toppled over had its guns been fired (p. 9). This report prompted the rebuilding of Fort San Marcos. The new fort encompassed portions of the old one, with an expanded area to the north. It was in this northern addition where we found the cedar posts still intact. Fortunately, maps of both of these San Marcos forts have survived (pp. 9 and 37). We learned from this project that the work of Major Osterhout had only slightly damaged the fort ruin. One day I hope to return to this fort to excavate the undisturbed area inside it to learn more of what lies beneath the soils of time.

An interpretive drawing of a sixteenth-century Spanish crossbowman by Darby Erd. Excavated at Santa Elena were: crossbow triggers and iron arrow points as well as the hooks that held the man's sword to his belt.

Chapter 9

The War at Fort San Felipe in 1576

From 1982 to 1984 my expeditions concentrated on the excavation of Fort San Felipe. In order to put these projects into perspective, I present in this chapter some historical background on the events taking place in 1576 having a direct bearing on Fort San Felipe and Santa Elena. The surviving Spanish documents are particularly rich and interesting from this year, during which time the Escamazu Indians attacked Fort San Felipe and burned Santa Elena in what has been called the "Escamazu War."

The general in charge of Fort San Felipe at Santa Elena in June of 1576 was Hernando de Miranda. He was said to be an uncouth man unfit to govern anything but cattle. The men often laughed at his orders. Ensign Hernando Moyano, however, followed orders to get food for the soldiers from Native American villages, taking twenty soldiers from Fort San Felipe with him.

In the village of Chief Orista they found a feast in progress. Moyano demanded food, but he was refused. He and his soldiers took the food anyway. An old chief asked Moyano why he came to make war and Moyano replied that he came only for food. The chief then asked why the soldiers had the fuses to their arquebuses lit and Moyano, to prove his good intentions, ordered the fuses extinguished. As soon as the fuses were put out, the soldier's guns were useless, and the Indians fell upon Moyano and his men and killed all of them except one.

Andrés Calderón had gone into the bushes to answer a call of nature when the attack came. With Indians behind him, he ran toward the water, jumped into it, and swam to Santa Elena. Some children saw the naked Calderón coming toward them from the marsh and assisted him into the city where "great was the weeping for the brothers, sons and husbands who had been killed."

39

The Native Americans cut off the heads of the twenty soldiers from Fort San Felipe and carried them as gifts to the chiefs of the Guale Indians, located south of Santa Elena, on what is now the Georgia coast. The victory over Moyano and his men gave courage to the Escamazu Indians and they soon began to converge on Santa Elena. Soon another group of soldiers under Captain Alonso de Solís were ordered to leave Fort San Felipe with war dogs and explore the island, which some of them considered foolish, but Captain Solís insisted, and these men too, were attacked and killed. Only a few wounded war dogs returned. All the Escamazu Indians in the area then arose in rebellion against the Spaniards. As the people at Santa Elena and Fort San Felipe watched, hundreds of Indians crossed in canoes to the island and attacked Fort San Felipe. The attack lasted about two hours until the attackers ran out of arrows. General Miranda gave orders to strengthen the fort, but many Spaniards wanted to leave.

There were only about seventeen soldiers, old men and young boys in the fort, along with some of the residents of Santa Elena, with "more than sixty women with their boy and girl children, shouting and crying from fear of the said Indians." The women pleaded with General Miranda "with great weeping and wailing," entreating him to leave Fort San Felipe and abandon Santa Elena. They said that their husbands had been killed and they wanted him to take them away from there, but he refused.

A few days after the attack, General Miranda had stayed up all night standing sentinel-watch with the few defenders of the fort and at dawn had fallen asleep. Thirty women entered his bedroom and before he could become fully awake, they seized his arms and legs and carried him to a vessel anchored nearby. He shouted for them to turn him loose, and gave orders and threatened punishment against them. The women, however, made it clear to him that if he did not abandon Santa Elena and the fort, they would throw him into the sea. They cut the mooring lines to the vessel so he couldn't get back on shore. He soon gave orders for the others to come aboard, and Santa Elena was abandoned. While they waited for the tide to rise to allow the vessel to clear the bar, they saw a large number of Indians set fire to Fort San Felipe and the houses of Santa Elena. The first Santa Elena was sacked and in ruins. Some of the survivors went to St. Augustine and others to Havana. Artifacts from this war are discussed in Chapters 13 and 15.

Chapter 10

A Bastion of Fort San Felipe Is Dug

In 1982 I received a grant from the National Endowment for the Humanities to excavate the northwest bastion of the Fort San Felipe. I knew from the drawing I had made when I discovered the fort (p. 16), that an excavation area measuring 50 by 60 feet would allow me to examine the northwest bastion to learn about its construction and to recover artifacts associated with it. No Spanish fort from this time period had ever been dug before, so we were interested to learn all we could about its construction. From documents, we knew that the moat was dug in 1574 and that Fort San Felipe was burned by Native Americans in 1576. We were interested in evidence of the burning of the fort and recovering objects from the moat dating from these two years.

Our previous work determined that a moat 16 feet wide by 5 feet deep surrounded the fort. The plan we drew in 1979 revealed that the east half of the fort had washed away, leaving the west side of the fort, measuring 200 feet from bastion to bastion and part of the moat along the north and south sides.

As we excavated and uncovered clues to the construction of the bastion, we found that the Spaniards had first dug a one-foot wide ditch to form a square bastion. In this ditch they placed a vertical palisade-post wall, probably around ten feet high. As they dug the moat around the outside of this palisade wall, they threw the dirt inside it to make the elevated bastion for an artillery piece.

Our excavations revealed that when the Indians attacked and burned the fort, the upright wall of the bastion had caught fire, and as the burning timbers lost their strength, the pressure of the sand inside the bastion forced the wall to collapse, causing the burning timbers to fall into the surrounding moat upside down, with sand spilling on top of them, scorching the sand and turning it an orange-red in color.

41

The northwest bastion of Fort San Felipe during excavation.

As excavation proceeded, a cannon ball of the size to fit a Spanish falcon artillery piece and a piece of armor were found in the edge of the moat, witnessing the military function the moat and the fort performed. As we dug, a raccoon family in an oak above our heads watched our activity with interest, as we did them.

When we excavated to the bottom of the moat, we found some of the trash that had been thrown from the bastion during its use, which we knew from the documents to be from 1574 to 1576. Spanish and American Indian pottery fragments were the primary objects recovered. In one place on the bottom of the moat, however, a cluster of lead balls for an arquebus was found lying together, probably representing a pouch fallen from a soldier's belt shortly after the moat was dug.

We discovered from the evidence of the burning timbers falling into the moat that the bottom of the moat when the fort burned was located two feet higher than it had been when originally excavated by the Spaniards in 1574. Two feet of erosional sand had washed into the bottom of the moat during its use by the Spaniards, turning it into a shallow ditch at the time the fort burned. We could understand this rapid erosion into the moat since we had witnessed, during our work, the remarkable amount of sand that could wash into the moat from a single summer storm. Obviously the Spaniards had more important worries than to spend time periodically cleaning out the moat ditch of Fort San Felipe.

Using the clues we found, we conducted documentary research to discover more about the San Felipe type of fort. We discovered that our data fit the description of earthen forts made of vertical posts set into ditches, forming walls, called parapets, to hold back dirt. Bundles of sticks, called faggots, and woven baskets holding earth, were also used in such short-term stick and dirt forts (p. 44).

44

A stack of faggots

Corner of a bastion

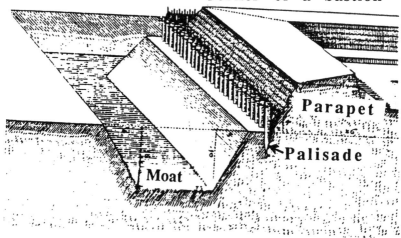

Parapet

Palisade

Moat

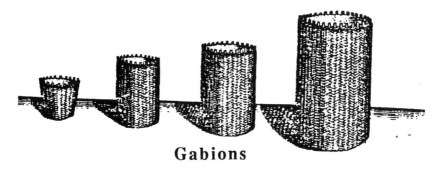

Gabions

A stack of faggots, moat, palisade and parapet, and various sizes of gabions (baskets filled with earth) used in the construction of forts of earth and wood such as Fort San Felipe. (Wilhelm Dilich, 1640, Pl. XIIV, XCV, XXIII Für die Reproduktionsgenehmigung danken wir der Bayerischen Staatsbibliothek München.)

Chapter 11

A Casa Fuerte Is Found

In 1983 and 1984, we excavated the entire interior of Fort San Felipe through a grant from the National Science Foundation. My goal in this project was to search for the *casas fuertes* or fortified houses we knew from documents to have been inside the area outlined by the moat and built prior to the fort. My crew and I stripped the topsoil from the entire area inside the fort. What we found was a narrow ditch outlining an area 50 by 70 feet, representing the location of the wall of one of the *casas fuertes*. This building, along with another fortified house, was constructed in 1572, and the moat and bastions were placed around it in 1574 to complete Fort San Felipe.

Sixteen large postholes, three to four feet across were discovered. Posts that had been in these holes formed the support for the second floor or platform for the building. The large size of the postholes indicated that large posts, supporting heavy weight were involved, suggesting artillery on a second floor level. I discovered that this fortified house was not built with square corners, but was in the shape of a parallelogram. Apparently, the person who laid out this building before the ditch was dug made an error at the corners, producing two acute angles and two obtuse angles for the building.

From the archaeology and the documents we found that Fort San Felipe was built in stages. First two fortified houses were built. The one we found was constructed by placing faggots upright like palisades in a 50 by 70 foot ditch to form a protective wall against possible attack by Native Americans while materials were being gathered inside. Faggots are bundles of sticks, about nine feet long, more easily gathered than larger palisade posts, that can be used as a defensive wall.

45

When the large timbers for the fort were ready, the Spaniards dug sixteen large holes to hold them. To dig these holes they had to remove some of the faggots from the ditch to allow the postholes to be dug and the posts to be placed in position. Horizontal beams were then placed across the top of the sixteen posts to form the base for the second floor artillery platform. The faggot wall formed the protection for the ground floor, with the second floor likely enclosed by boards to protect the defenders during attack.

Two years later, to provide additional protection, the four-bastioned, trapezoidal-shaped fort moat was laid out around the two *casas fuertes*, with a palisade placed in a ditch paralleling the inside edge of the moat, a few feet from it. Dirt from digging the moat was thrown behind the palisade wall to form a parapet, which is an embankment of earth. Faggot bundles of sticks and basketry gabions filled with earth, standard fort-building materials at the time, were likely used as well (p. 44).

This information about Fort San Felipe did not come easy, but required much digging, and sifting, and mapping, and piecing together of the complex archaeological puzzle. I will attempt to explain the sometimes confusing puzzle-solving process I faced as I "read the dirt" of Fort San Felipe's ruins.

The large postholes were the largest I had seen and were also the most fascinating to "read" and interpret in profile. Fortunately there were sixteen such postholes and I looked at several in detail and found the same pattern present in each one. What we saw, when we sliced the postholes in two vertically, was that there was an offset, or stepped-off area to the side. Such a shape was caused, I believe, when the posts being installed in the hole were so large that an off-set, something like a ramp, was necessary to allow the base of the large post to slide more easily into the hole. This indicated that large posts were placed in the holes.

The sides of the bottom of the hole contained dark humus, such as that accumulating when leaves are allowed to rot in a hole. This suggests that after the posts were in place, the holes remained open for some time, allowing the introduction of leaves in the bottom around the post. I think this period of time was during the construction of the fortified house, when the horizontal beams resting on each post were being placed into the rigid framework for the *casa fuerte* platform. This explains the humus seen around the outer edge of the bottom of the postholes.

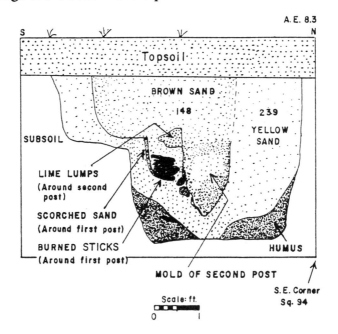

Profile drawing and photograph of a casa fuerte posthole.

In each posthole, a short distance up from the bottom of the hole, a crescent-shaped charcoal concentration, made up of small burned sticks about the size of a finger, was seen. This phenomenon, present in all the postholes we examined, must be explained. I discovered that the charcoal crescent had once been a circle of sticks around the original large post and that when the small sticks burned they left a circular charcoal ring around the original post, scorching the sand next to it (p. 47).

My interpretation of this part of the profile is that the small crescent of charcoal sticks represents faggots placed around the large posts to keep sand from coming in contact with the large posts. We learn from documents that the Spaniards knew that "sand rots wood." The faggot bundles removed from the ditch while the holes were dug were placed around each post to isolate it from the sand to help prevent the posts from rotting. When Fort San Felipe was burned in 1576, the faggots around each post caught fire and burned down around the post.

Another pattern I observed in the postholes was that in each case the charcoal crescent had been cut into when a smaller post was put into place. This was revealed to me by the presence of the postmold of this smaller post (p. 47). This second post, placed in the hole after the first post had been removed, did not touch the bottom of the hole. A postmold is an impression left in a posthole by a post as it rotted or was burned in place.

I interpret this second series of postmolds as being the remains of a building with posts occupying the same postholes as the original *casa fuerte* posts. The people placing these posts in the holes had to know where each hole was located. This would mean that someone saw the ruin of the *casa fuerte* and removed the burned posts from the holes and placed new posts in the same holes. The new posts were smaller and not set as deeply into the hole as the original posts had been.

Another set of clues associated with the second set of postmolds was the fact that around each of these later postmolds there had been placed a quantity of lime lumps. I interpret these lumps as an attempt to keep sand away from the wooden posts to help prevent the posts from rotting.

The interpretation of these archaeological posthole and postmold data ties in closely to some documentary information we have relating to the history of Fort San Felipe. The year after the fort was burned by Native Americans, Pedro Menéndez Marqués came to Santa Elena and built a blockhouse to the north of where he built Fort San Marcos. It is my interpretation that he saw the ruins of Fort San Felipe, removed the burned posts from the postholes, and placed new ones in the same holes in order to build his blockhouse. This would explain the archaeological data we found.

We also discovered three wells inside Fort San Felipe that furnished water for the soldiers. These special, large, complicated features will be discussed in the next chapter.

A number of ditches were found inside the fort that were not dug by the Spaniards occupying it. These were plumbing ditches, some with cast iron pipes still in them, used by the United States Marine Corps when they had barracks buildings on the site during the first World War. We also found the footing holes for these barracks, which damaged the Spanish information in only a few places.

The excavation of the northwest bastion and the interior of the fort has given us a far better picture of Fort San Felipe than had ever been obtained from documents alone, since no map or description of the fort has yet been found. I discovered, for instance, that the fort was not the square configuration one might expect, but was a trapezoidal shape, with the long side facing the water where more guns could be arrayed for defense. A 1593 map of a fort at St. Augustine with this shape has survived.

Although only half of Fort San Felipe has survived the elements of the past four hundred years, I was able to draw a map of Fort San Felipe based on our archaeological information (p. 50). I hope to return to Fort San Felipe some day to excavate the moat along the west and south sides of the fort.

50

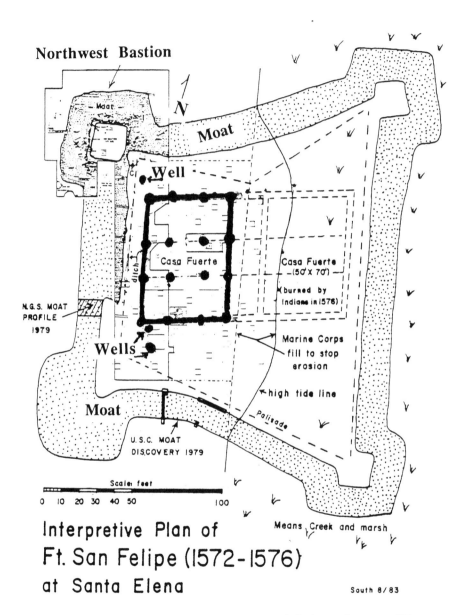

Interpretive Plan of
Ft. San Felipe (1572-1576)
at Santa Elena

South 8/83

The archaeological drawing of the trapezoidal shaped moat of Fort San Felipe, showing the casa fuerte ditch and postholes inside. The east half of the fort has been eroded away by storms.

Chapter 12

Digging Fort San Felipe's Wells

Near the throat of the northwest bastion a doughnut-shaped filled-in hole was seen in our 1983 excavation. Another was found just outside the southwest corner of the *casa fuerte*. I interpreted these holes as wells, though some of my crew were skeptical. My identification of these holes came from the fact that when holes are dug deeply into a site they tap the differently colored soil lying deeper in the ground and when this soil is thrown back into the hole it contrasts dramatically in color with the soil lying nearer the surface. The outer ring for the doughnut-shaped feature was flecked with white sand not found near the surface, telling me that the feature was deep.

Doughnut shaped features are characteristic of wells, with a uniformly dark central stain resulting from the central shaft of the well as it filled up after the well was abandoned. This dark center is surrounded by an outer ring containing the flecks of lighter soil thrown back into the hole outside the central barrel-liner of the well. It is, therefore, highly predictable, that such doughnut shaped features seen near the surface, will turn out to be wells when excavated.

In excavating the three Fort San Felipe wells I used a backhoe to cut a deep working shaft beside the doughnut shaped hole. I then excavated the well *from the side*. This allowed the well shaft to be sliced vertically. I always excavate a well in one foot levels while separating the contents of the outer ring from the inner well shaft, assigning a control number to the outer "doughnut" part of the well hole, and another to the darker inner column of soil. This allows me to separate the outer doughnut, which represents the soil and objects thrown in around barrels forming the well shaft *at the time the well was dug*, from the darker central shaft representing the soil and objects accumulated in the well *after it was abandoned*.

51

52

Bill Hunt cleaning a doughnut-shaped well hole in Fort San Felipe prior to excavating it from the side. The vertical profile of the well with the top of the wooden barrel liner is seen near the bottom.

Because different time periods are involved in the inner shaft and the outer backfilled ring, the artifacts recovered from the two parts of the well allow us to differentiate the date when the well was dug from the date it was abandoned.

Far more artifacts are usually recovered from the inner well shaft than from the outer ring since the inner shaft is an artifact trap for things accumulated around and in the well during and after its use. The outer doughnut shaft, however, quite often might contain only a few artifacts that were lying around before the well was dug. If the well site area was not occupied prior to the well having been dug, no artifacts are likely to be found in the outer shaft.

Wells are excellent object-traps for recovering biological specimens such as leaves, seeds, etc. that have survived 400 years in the oxygen free atmosphere below the water table. Such items are not often seen by archaeologists elsewhere on the site. Among those things preserved by the cool water inside the barrels of Fort San Felipe were insect wings, tendrils of vine, and a piece of cloth. Seeds of squash, pumpkin, watermelon and persimmon were recovered, along with the egg case of a roach once living in the Spanish *casa fuerte* or on the walls of the well. Cockleburs, cane, and a piece of rope were also recovered from one of the wells, all clues to the daily lives of those inside Fort San Felipe.

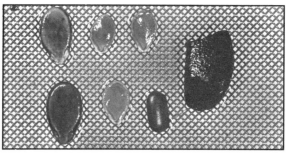

Recovered from a well in Fort San Felipe were: watermelon , squash, and persimmon seeds, and a roach egg case.

Of particular interest was a piece of cloth torn into a strip. When Native Americans were attacking Fort San Felipe in 1576, all the sheets in Santa Elena were torn into strips to make fuses for the arquebuses, because all the match rope usually used for that purpose had been used up.

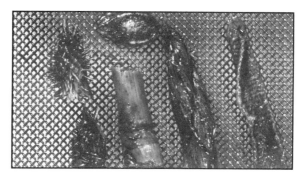

Also found in a Fort San Felipe well were: Cockleburs, pumpkin seed, cane, a piece of braided rope and a strip of woven sheeting. Such strips were torn from the sheets of Santa Elena residents to be used for arquebus fuses during the attack on Fort San Felipe by Native Americans in 1576.

54

Not far south of the well at the southwest corner of the *casa fuerte* ruin, a n oystershell-filled well was located. This well had been used for a while, but it had been dug slightly below the water table, so it soon became unusable. The barrel liners had been removed when it was abandoned, and the hole then used to dispose of oystershell garbage and other trash.

An abandoned Fort San Felilpe well filled with oystershells.

One of the most interesting objects found in this well was the spout of a Ming Dynasty porcelain wine ewer, an item of such cost that it may well have once belonged to the founder of Santa Elena, Pedro Menéndez de Avilés, himself. Porcelain was so rare it was worth three times its weight in silver, so only the wealthy could afford to own it.

A reconstructive drawing of a Ming Dynasty porcelain wine ewer, from a spout fragment recovered from the abandoned well in Fort San Felipe.

Chapter 13

Learning From Military Objects Found in Fort San Felipe

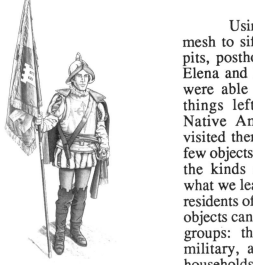

Using screens with 1/8th inch mesh to sift the soil taken from the pits, postholes and ditches at Santa Elena and her forts, my crew and I were able to recover thousands of things left by the Spaniards and Native Americans who lived and visited there. I will discuss only a few objects in this volume to illustrate the kinds of things we found and what we learned from them about the residents of Santa Elena. The Spanish objects can easily be divided into two groups: those that were used by the military, and those from domestic households. In this chapter I discuss some of the Spanish military objects and in the next chapter I illustrate the domestic artifacts we found.

Some objects, such as lead shot, can be identified as likely having served a military function. Some of these frequently recovered artifacts showed human teeth marks, as though chewed by a nervous soldier.

Teeth marks on a lead ball from Fort San Felipe.

Some lead shot had been fired, striking some object, distorting them from the impact. Many pieces of sprue were also found. A single bullet mold, such as those found at Santa Elena,

56

would mold one bullet at a time, but gang-molds casting six bullets at a time were present in the town since we found sprue sows (the lead bar left after the shot were cut away) showing six shots had been cut off. When the cast lead shot were cut away with nippers, the sprue was often discarded, to be recovered by us four hundred years later.

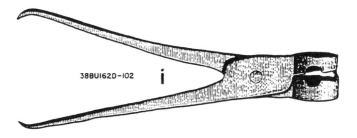

A drawing of one of the bullet molds found in Santa Elena.

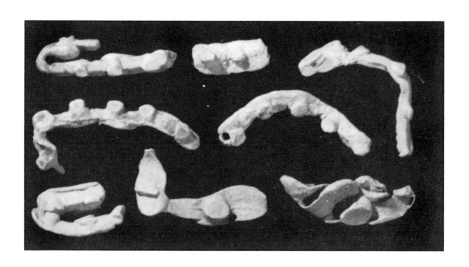

Lead sprue and sows from Santa Elena and Fort San Felipe

The guns that fired the lead balls were known as arquebuses or "mosquetes," each having a five foot barrel and a 3/4 inch bore. One lead ball of this diameter was recovered in our excavations. An arquebus could fire several smaller balls at a time. This practice apparently was preferred at Santa Elena and Fort San Felipe, over 300 such balls having been recovered. Light arquebuses could hit a playing card at 70 yards and kill a deer beyond 100, while heavier ones could pierce armor at 200 yards.

The weapon was fired by dipping a glowing match or fuse made of rope into powder by depressing a trigger. Triggers of these guns were recovered in our digging. An "S" shaped match holder, called a serpentine, held the fuse and dipped it into the powder when the trigger was pulled. Fragments of arquebus serpentines were found by us at the northwest bastion of Fort San Felipe.

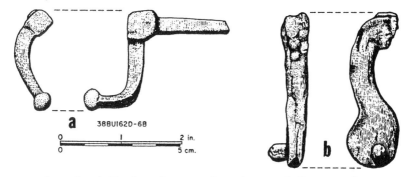

An end and side view of an arquebus trigger and of a serpentine.

Although Spaniards had developed a rifled gun almost two decades before Santa Elena was founded, no rifled lead balls were found by us. The reason the Spaniards did not continue to use rifled guns is seen in an interesting story found in the documents.

A bishop was interested in determining whether the new rifled guns were as good in hitting targets as the arquebus. In a test, appropriately blessed silver bullets, known to be effective against witches and werewolves, were shot from rifled barrels. These were matched against lead balls not having the benefit of blessing, fired from non-rifled guns, at a target 200 meters away. Not one silver bullet hit the target, while 19 of the 20 lead balls did. To the bishop, this test cast doubt on the rifling.

58

An explanation from the documents regarding the rifled gun experiment, sheds light on the thought processes of the Spaniards at the time. "Some held that tiny imps, who delighted in misdirecting a good Christian's bullet, could not keep their seats on a spinning ball" (Trench 1972:107). Others argued that imps riding on lead balls were beneficial, causing the ball to fly more truly. The soldiers at Fort San Felipe, using arquebuses and good crossbows, however, did not have to worry about imps losing their seats since no rifled guns were in use at the time.

The crossbow is a weapon that, by two hundred years before Santa Elena, had a range of about 450 yards. It was considered such a dreaded weapon that various Papal edicts forbade its use against Christians, but it was a popular military and hunting weapon for hundreds of years until replaced by increasingly popular firearms, sometime after the period of Santa Elena. Crossbow triggers were found at Santa Elena.

A crossbowman (Payne-Gallwey).

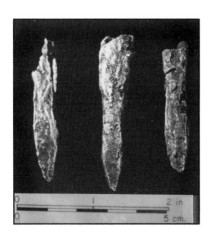

Crossbow arrowheads.

Eight iron arrow points from crossbow arrows, or quarrels, were recovered from inside Fort San Felipe. None were found in the domestic occupation area of Santa Elena. In Spain, poisoned crossbow points were used in hunting game. At Santa Elena, the only crossbows were apparently in the hands of the soldiers.

The crossbows had such a powerful bow that special devices were necessary to cock them. A goat's-foot lever allowed the crossbow to be cocked quickly, drawing back the powerful bow with a claw-frame. The pressure was so great that the goat's-foot lever sometimes was bent or destroyed in the process. Several damaged pieces of goat's-foot levers were found in Fort San Felipe.

A bow-string claw from a goat's-foot lever from Fort San Felipe. Two of these were mounted on a claw-frame which pulled on the crossbow string to cock the bow.

Another military item recovered from the ruins was the brass serpent head from a sword handle. Although swords were in the hands of the military at Fort San Felipe, this brass serpent head is the only clue we have found of their presence in the fort. Swords, like most valuable things were carefully kept by owners.

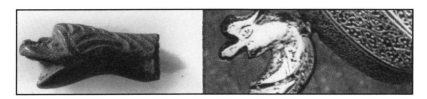

A brass serpent head from Fort San Felipe thought to be from a sword hilt such as that seen in a detail from a photograph of a rapier from the mid-sixteenth century. (From Schöbel 1975. Courtesy Historisches Museum, Dresden, Germany.)

Drawing of a pike point.

One iron pike point was recovered. Three dozen pikes were mentioned in Flores' inspection of Fort San Marcos in 1578.

60

A piece of armor with a brass buckle attached also was found in Fort San Felipe, along with brass armor hinges and buckles. These objects are representative of personal iron armor plate in use during the 16th century.

A piece of Spanish armor with a brass buckle attached is uncovered by Michael Hartley in the northwest bastion of Fort San Felipe.

More popular at Fort San Felipe, however, were more comfortable quilted armor coats called *escaupiles*. Such coats had protective copper or brass discs with a central hole, sewn between layers of canvas, creating a quilted appearance. Such armored garments are sometimes called jackcoats.

A brass disc from a quilted coat of armor called an escaupile.

These coats were much in evidence in Santa Elena and her forts. When Flores inspected Fort San Marcos in 1578, he found "eighty *escaupiles*," all hanging on nails.

A witness said in 1570 that the soldiers at St. Augustine had taken their *escaupiles* apart so they could be used as shirts. It may well be that they then traded the brass discs to Native Americans, because a number of similar discs have been found with Indian burials. At Santa Elena in the same year, it was said that among the fifty soldiers in the fort, there were not six shirts, which reveals the need for shirts and the reason for taking their *escaupiles* apart to make two shirts of the inner and outer linings.

Many military things mentioned in documents were not recovered by our excavations. Cannons, swords, cutlasses, helmets, and other items are known to have been present at Fort San Felipe, but we have not found them so far. One object we uncovered inside Fort San Felipe did not appear to be military until after it was X-rayed and research was conducted to place it in context. It was a crescent-shaped iron object, four and one-half inches across, that appeared to be two crescents lying together. The X-rays showed holes along the inside of the crescent and a hinged joint at the ends. Research revealed that it was the iron frame of a bandolier bag, used by a soldier to hold his lead balls and other equipment for firing his arquebus. String sewn through the holes held the bag to the crescent shaped frame. Such a bag is seen in the 1548 painting of Charles V of Spain by Titian. This finding clearly placed this object, not in the classification with domestic items, as a purse would be, but with the military objects.

The military objects that were recovered at Fort San Felipe, Fort San Marcos and Santa Elena reveal the need for defense of the settlement by the Spaniards living there. The Spanish weapons contrast with the wooden clubs and bow and fire arrows the Native Americans are known to have used to repel the Spanish interlopers on their homeland. Given the power and awe-inspiring nature of the crossbow, the arquebus, the sword, and the bronze artillery pieces in the bastions at Santa Elena's forts, it is remarkable that the Native Americans were able to drive the Spaniards from the city of Santa Elena and sack it in 1576.

The iron top of the bandolier bag used to hold lead shot and other supplies for the arquebus is illustrated in this 1548 painting by Titian of King Charles V of Spain. ("Charles V at the Battle of Muhlberg," from Hamlyn 1970:68. Courtesy of Museo del Prado, Madrid.)

Chapter 14

Domestic Objects Found in Santa Elena

Besides the military objects left by the Spaniards at Santa Elena and her forts, there were a large number of domestic objects found. A few of the categories of objects recovered will be discussed in this chapter to give the reader some knowledge of the daily life of Santa Elena's residents not provided by the documents that have survived. Personal items, such as buttons and charms, thimbles and pins, are not the things mentioned by those who wrote the official documents and letters that historians read to reconstruct histories. They are the stuff of daily life, familiar to every resident of Santa Elena, that only archaeology can provide.

Second only to eggshells as the most fragile objects recovered were pieces of very thin, delicate fragments of Spanish glassware, representing tumblers, decanters and wine glasses, some of which had milk white stripes. Some of these are as thin as lightbulb glass. Not everyone in Santa Elena could afford to own and transport such fragile objects to America.

Striped glass fragments from a decanter such as illustrated in a detail from a still-life, "Bodegón" by Juan Van der Hamen, around 1622. (From Lopez-Rey 1968: Plate 35. Courtesy of Museo del Prado, Madrid.)

64

    We also recovered large amounts of pottery from Spain, Italy, Mexico and China, reflecting the world trade network in operation in Spain during the sixteenth century. Two large forms of containers were olive jars and basins. Olive jars were used to store oil, honey, water, and anything else that needed to be stored (p. 14). They were relatively sturdy and would survive ocean voyages in the holds of ships. Large green glazed earthenware basins larger than bicycle wheels were used in Santa Elena. These basins were used as we use wash tubs, for laundry, for baths and for storage. Similar earthenware vessels are still being made in Spain.

    Majolica is the name for the type of pottery used in Santa Elena as tableware. It has a white tin-ash glaze and is often painted with cobalt blue, or purple designs. The most frequent forms found at Santa Elena were bowls, plates and pitchers. Paintings from the sixteenth century show this type pottery, and we matched the types of pottery shown, with the fragments we found.

This Santo Domingo Blue on White majolica pitcher broke when it was dropped into a well in Fort San Felipe. A similar pitcher is shown in a detail from a Spanish painting by Diego Rodriguez de Silva y Velázquez, "The Servant," probably 1618-22. (Courtesy Sir Alfred Beit, London. Photo courtesy of The Art Institute of Chicago.)

Santa Elena Mottled Blue on White.

Because some of the majolica wares found at Santa Elena have not been described in the literature prior to our discovery of them, I have given them names relating to the Santa Elena site. A blotchy blue majolica ware I have called "Santa Elena Mottled Blue on White majolica." A type having a white glaze on the interior and a green lead glaze on the exterior I have called, "Santa Elena Green and White majolica". A green-edged majolica type I call "San Felipe Green-edged majolica."

The most colorful majolica pottery found at Santa Elena was made in Italy and is known as Montelupo Polychrome majolica. Another type of 16th century Italian pottery is a dark blue on a lighter blue color and is known as Ligurian Blue on Blue majolica.

A Mexican red painted relief-molded ware we found is known as Aztec Red Ware, though it may be Maya pottery from Yucatan. Some pieces of this earthenware have feathers in relief. These fragments may be from a vessel depicting Quetzalquoatl, the traditional feathered serpent god of Mexico.

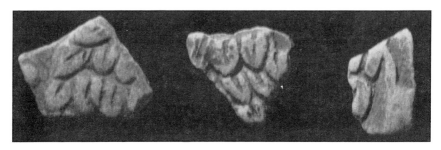

Feather-decorated Mexican Red Painted Aztec pottery from Santa Elena and Fort San Felipe, reflecting the Spanish connection with Mexico. Such wares were shipped to Spain and to her colonial settlements such as Santa Elena.

The most sophisticated ceramic production in the world in the sixteenth century was Chinese porcelain of the Wan Li Period of the Ming Dynasty. Spanish merchants, with the aid of overseas Chinese entrepreneurs, began to supply the Spanish empire with the produce of China and the Orient in exchange for New World silver. Within ten years of the establishment of Santa Elena, the Spanish empire had grown to include the Philippine archipelago in Southeast Asia. Goods flowed by way of Manila galleons across the Pacific Ocean to Acapulco, Mexico, where they were packed overland to Veracruz, and from there carried by ship through the Gulf of Mexico to Spain. Santa Elena, as part of this world system, received its share of these materials which included Ming Dynasty Chinese export porcelain. Cups, bowls, plates, and ginger jar forms of Ming porcelain were found at Santa Elena, as well as the spout of a wine ewer (p. 54).

We move from elite porcelain, to functional nails, found in abundance in Santa Elena and Fort San Felipe. A total of 1,367 nails and spikes, some one foot in length, were found in Santa Elena, 911 came from Fort San Felipe. Although rusted, they survived four hundred years in the soil of Parris Island. A group of large headed tacks was found, and I discovered through research that these were used to hold the wickerwork mats holding cargo in place aboard vessels bringing goods to the New World.

Nails identical to the ones recovered at Santa Elena are illustrated in paintings by sixteenth century artists. The nails are often painted in connection with the crucifixion of Christ, such as "The Dead Christ" by Annibale Carracci, which is the artist's sixteenth century rendition of the nails used to fasten Christ to the cross.

The paintings of the nails used to fasten Christ to the cross remind me of the individual I consider to be the mother of historical archaeology, Santa Elena (St. Helena in English), the mother of Constantine the Great, who lived during the fourth century. The Spaniards named their capital Santa Elena because they discovered the area on the day named for her. She is connected with nails because she dug at Golgotha, around A.D. 324, at the age of 80, and located nails she thought were those used to nail Christ to the cross. She was sainted by the Catholic Church for her excavations, and for discovery of the nails and fragments of the cross (Ferguson 1958). It is fitting, it seems to me, that historical archaeology has been carried out at a place named for her.

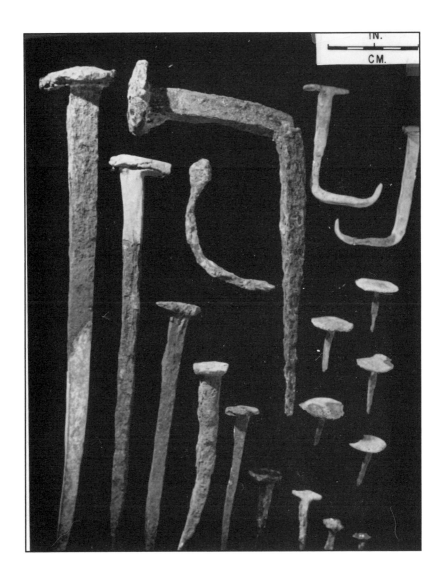

Blacksmith wrought nails from Santa Elena and Fort San Felipe.

68

Architectural items, such as nails and shutter and door hinge staples, and pintles and latches for securing doors and shutters, were found in both domestic and military contexts. Fired clay daub and oystershell plaster, also architectural remains, were found in some quantity at Santa Elena where houses once stood.

Furniture was represented by iron caselocks and small brass tacks and rivets as well as large domed brass tacks used to hold leather onto wooden stools and other furniture. From the scarcity of furniture hardware at Santa Elena it is apparent that household furniture at that time was likely simple and unadorned with metal fastenings, leaving few archaeological remains as witness to its presence.

An iron caselock for a chest and an iron buckle. All four corners of the lock have been torn out, indicating that great force was used to tear the lock away from the chest.

Among the interesting clothing hardware used by the residents of Santa Elena are iron buckles and hooks for holding sword carriers, and ball buttons and copper aglets, called lacing tips, used to lace sleeves to bodices. Some of the ball buttons were gold plated. These buttons are like the round ones shown on the clothing of Pedro Menéndez, founder of Santa Elena (p. 69), and on a lady's clothing (p. 71).

Portrait of Pedro Menéndez de Avilés, founder of Santa Elena and ball buttons like the ones shown on his garment. (Engraving courtesy of the Florida Historical Society.)

A number of copper stars were made at Santa Elena but their function is not entirely known. They may have been used on a whip used by religious devotees to flagellate themselves to draw blood to prove their love of Christ. Such stars are shown on the end of a flagellant's whip illustrated in a drawing by Tobias Stimmer, dating from 1570, during the period of Santa Elena's occupation.

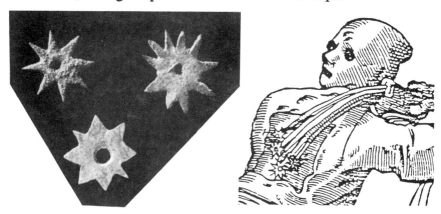

Copper stars from Santa Elena and a whip (with stars on the ends of thongs) being used to flagellate the back. (From "The Ecclesiastical Hierarchy" by Tobias Stimmer, around 1570. Cut by L. Fry, Vienna, 263, 1957. From Strauss 1975, Vol. 3:1056, Fig. 75. Courtesy Abaris Books, Inc., New York.)

70

Straight pins and thimbles as well as scissors used in tailoring are characteristic objects discarded and lost at Santa Elena's houses. The tailor at Santa Elena was Alonso de Olmos, who, with his wife, his mother-in-law, six children and a boarder, had a busy household. His family helped him in the tailoring business, and in raising hogs and planting corn. He also loaned money to his neighbors, sold dry goods from his tailor shop, and operated a tavern for the refreshment and entertainment of the community.

 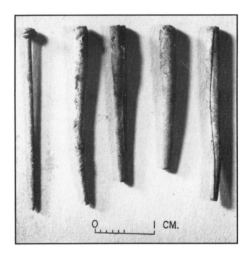

A brass thimble, a straight pin, and copper aglets (lacing tips), are reminders of the tailor, Olmos, who made clothing at Santa Elena.

In February 1572, Olmos and his attorney, Francisco Ruiz were ordered to assist in work on Fort San Felipe, but Olmos was busy. It was corn planting time, he said, and besides, he was not subject to military command. He refused. In a heated discussion on the matter, both Olmos and his attorney were knocked down by Governor Velasco and a gallows was ordered to be made to hang them. The Jesuit priests spoke in their behalf and both were spared. But they were chained to the fort and forced to help with its construction.

The clothing of the wealthy members of the Menéndez family and others far more affluent than the soldiers and most Spaniards in Santa Elena, was covered with a braid or embroidery, called *bordado,* similar to that seen on toreador's outfits today.

Many pieces of this border were found in our excavations. Most were of copper wire. One was of gold wire in a star-like pattern.

We also found some bordado of string, preserved by copper salts from a piece of copper associated with it. One piece of bordado had a faceted garnet bead fastened among the wire. Although Santa Elena was a frontier city in the 1560s, it was the capital of Spanish Florida, and the home of Menéndez and his family, and elegance of dress was seen in their homes.

Gold star-shaped bordado wire and copper bordado from Santa Elena. Bordado on a lady's costume. From "Queen Isabel" by Velazquez and assistant, around 1632. (Courtesy Kunsthistorisches Museum, Vienna. From Lopez Rey 1968: Plate 161.) Notice the ball buttons fastening the front of the lady's dress.

Many personal items were recovered from our screening, such as carved religious objects made of jet, a type of petrified wood, designed to be sewn onto clothing. One of these was a triple clinched fist, or "figa," symbolizing the hand of God holding the souls of the saved. It was designed to repel the evil eye and thought to have the power to repel bullets. Another type of jet ornament had three lobes, symbolizing the Father, the Son and the Holy Ghost.

72

A triple figa and a trilobate ornament such as that worn on the necklace of a lady in "La Purificación" by de León Picardo painted in the second quarter of the Sixteenth Century. (From Angulo 1954: 115, Fig. 114. Courtesy of the Museo del Prado, Madrid.)

An earring of glass was also recovered, and a lady wearing an identical, tear shaped earring is seen in a 1555 painting hanging in the Cathedral of Seville, Spain. Another jet ornament in the shape of a scallop shell was found in Fort San Felipe. The scallop shell is connected with St. James, the patron saint of Spain.

Part of a glass earring like the one worn in a detail from the painting "Santas Justa y Rufina y San Lucas" by Fernando Storm around 1555. A scallop shell ornament symbolic of St. James, the patron saint of Spain. (Courtesy of Catedral de Sevilla. From Angulo 1954: 213, Fig. 219.)

Six glass beads and one of garnet have been recovered in Spanish pits in Fort San Felipe, but none has yet been found in association with Santa Elena's homes. Eight Native American disc shell beads were discovered in Santa Elena and twenty in Fort San Felipe, witness to the contact of cultures (p. 80).

A brass Maltese cross with the relief figure of Christ reflects the presence of the Catholic church at Santa Elena. Although a church existed in the town, we have not yet identified either the church building or the associated cemetery. This Maltese cross is the insignia of the Knights of Malta, a high order in the Roman Catholic Church.

Coins are also personal items. Five were recovered from our excavations. Three are copper maravedíes, a low denomination coin, and the fourth is a silver real. The fifth, a silver blob stamped on one side with the arms of Spain, is a unique coin in the history of coinage in America and may have been melted and struck at Santa Elena. Other parts of melted silver coins we found tend to support this idea.

38BUI62E-24A

A copper maravedí coin.

A broken Maltese cross similar to one seen in a detail from the painting "Alof de Wignacourt, with a Page" by Caravaggio (From Metropolitan Museum of Art 1985:331. Courtesy of Musée du Louvre, Paris.) A unique silver coin probably struck in Santa Elena.

Bone dice were recovered from Santa Elena. Among sixteenth century painters, dice were depicted as symbolic of the passion of Christ. The fickleness of fate was also symbolized by dice. Breaking dice in two symbolized a contract between individuals or a renewal of friendship as the split die halves try to rejoin. In the sixteenth century, fortune telling charts could indicate, with three dice, how an individual's fate and future could be determined. We found two half-dies at Santa Elena, as well as a whole one. Documents say that soldiers spent a lot of time gambling, as some do today. Pottery discs, interpreted by archaeologists as gaming devices, made of both Indian and Spanish olive jar pottery at Santa Elena, also likely were used for gambling.

A bone die, a gaming disc made from a Spanish olive jar sherd, and a gaming disc made from Native American pottery, probably used in gambling.

A number of activities are reflected by the worked copper and brass we recovered and an iron anvil used in metalworking. Kettles apparently were being cut and reworked into new objects. Bone awls suggest basketworking. Iron chisels, wedges and gouges were used for woodworking and for trade with Native Americans. A number of broken twist-type auger bits with broken shafts are witness to the need to drill holes in timbers to fasten them together. This process took great strength, and a number of the heavy drill bits were twisted in two by the Spaniards and had to be discarded. Lead fishline weights and iron fishhooks relate to the heavy dependence at Santa Elena on the streams and rivers to sustain life, since imported food was always scarce and the people were often hungry.

An anchor fluke fragment is testimony to connection with the sea, which was a main highway as well as a source of food. Whaling may well have been carried out at Santa Elena, since we found in Fort San Felipe, a flensing knife used to strip blubber from whales, an activity pursued by Spaniards from the Basque Provinces of Spain at this time. Among Pedro Menéndez de Avilés' goods in Fort San Felipe on March 23, 1576, were two large copper vessels (ollas) "to render whale blubber," the documents state. The whaling items only may have been stored at Fort San Felipe, but they also may reveal whaling activity at Santa Elena.

This summary of clues to the Spanish past in Santa Elena through my archaeological work has illustrated only a few of the involvements and details of domestic life there. The broader picture from a theoretical and socio-economic perspective has been published elsewhere. There are many questions I am asking about the life and activities of the residents of Santa Elena and the Native Americans they dealt with daily. In my search for answers I have learned much as I stepped through the archaeological doorway to the past at Santa Elena and her forts. I used a scientific archaeological approach requiring the counting of the bits and pieces of pottery and other things to determine the frequent contact between the Spanish colonists and the Native Americans. I have identified patterned relationships between the house ruins and the objects scattered around them to determine the function and economic level of the occupants of the houses.

I have compared the military objects with the domestic objects, and the more costly objects with the cheaper items, in relation to where they were found, in order to try to get a better understanding of the different social and economic levels present in Santa Elena and her forts. A pit containing mostly pig bones, chicken bones, bordado and porcelain fragments, for instance, is interpreted quite differently from one containing no pig bones, no porcelain, and no expensive bordado. It is from such contrasting data that we interpret what went on in the past.

Chester DePratter drawing the position of pig bones discarded in one of the daub processing pits beside a house ruin in Santa Elena. In such garbage disposal pits are found most of the domestic objects thrown from Spanish houses.

Chapter 15

Finding Native American Clues

Santa Elena was a frontier settlement and as such had much contact with Native Americans. In the closest Native American village were Escamazu Indians, also referred to as the Indians of Santa Elena. South of Santa Elena, on the Georgia coast, were the Guale Indians, allies of the Escamaczu. One of our goals at Santa Elena was to find clues to the interactions between Native Americans and the Spaniards. We expected to find Native American cultural remains in the settlement as the result of social relationships, trade exchange, and military attack.

Exchange of items of material culture was carried out as Spanish soldiers took Native American wives and concubines. Archaeologist Kathleen Deagan points out that among the 1200 men who arrived in St. Augustine with Menéndez in 1565, only one hundred brought their wives. In 1578, a request was made for three hundred more men and only six women to be sent to *La Florida,* implying that many of the men may have found mates among Native American women. Liaisons between Spanish men and Native American women were formed throughout the Spanish New World, and Santa Elena was no exception. The result was that Santa Elena, no doubt, had a number of Native American residents and their mestizo children.

Throughout the excavations at Santa Elena and her forts I found Native American pottery. In the town of Santa Elena there was as much locally made ware as Spanish pottery, indicating the accessibility of locally made wares.

This Native American pottery was characteristically incised and stamped with a carved paddle line-block motif. Many pieces of the Native American vessels we recovered from Santa Elena refuse pits were coated on the exterior with soot and carbon, with burned food residue on the interior. Obviously, local pottery was being used as cooking vessels to prepare daily meals in Santa Elena.

An incised Native American pot from Santa Elena. Spaniards used these vessels for cooking their meals. By comparison, only a few Spanish redware cooking pot fragments have been recovered in excavations at Santa Elena and Fort San Felipe.

In contrast to the brown, sand-tempered paste seen in locally manufactured vessels, another type of Native American pottery was a chalky-paste ware with a black interior and light gray exterior. This chalky imported pottery, known as St. Johns ware, was made by the Timucua Indians in the St. Johns River area of northeast Florida. It was found broken in some quantity in the garbage dumps of Santa Elena's houses, but was virtually absent from Fort San Felipe. An explanation for this phenomenon may be related to time. Because Santa Elena's domestic household area reflects occupation during two decades, from 1566 to 1587, it could be that St. Johns pottery came into Santa Elena mainly after Fort San Felipe was burned in 1576, and thus it was only slightly represented there.

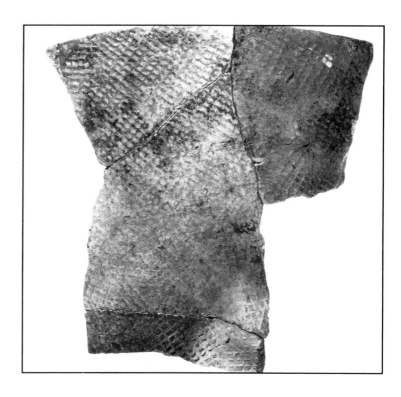

A rim sherd of St. John's Check Stamped pottery made by Timucua Indians near St. Augustine and imported into Santa Elena.

Eighty percent of the artifacts from the northwest bastion of Fort San Felipe were of Indian manufacture. The high percentage of Native American pottery in Fort San Felipe may have resulted from the payment of tribute by local Indians to the Spaniards in the fort. Historical documents frequently mention the Spaniards obtaining food from the Native Americans through forced tribute to Spanish officials at Santa Elena. Such tribute in the form of corn and other foodstuffs may well have been brought into the fort as the official center for paying tribute. Soldiers likely used the locally made vessels as cooking pots for preparing their meals.

The use of tobacco in Santa Elena, is seen in tobacco pipes of Native American manufacture. These are boat-shaped pipes characteristic of the area. I suspect the Spaniards used tobacco in the form of cigars, which they learned from the Indians.

80

Tobacco pipe fragments of Native American manufacture. A sixteenth century engraving by De Bry of a Le Moyne watercolor illustrates an Indian smoking a pipe.

Additional evidence for the close contact between Santa Elena's people and Native Americans was the presence of Indian made beads. Eight shell beads of Native American manufacture were recovered during the excavation of the domestic refuse deposits in Santa Elena, while twenty were found in Fort San Felipe.

Shell beads of Native American manufacture from Santa Elena.

The archaeology reveals, through the presence of Indian made shell beads and pottery, a far friendlier interaction between local Native Americans with Santa Elena's residents and soldiers during the first decade at Santa Elena than in the second.

Militant demands for food made by Santa Elena soldiers (Moyano and his men) on the closest Native American village resulted in the soldiers' deaths in 1576. These same neighboring Escamazu Indians were responsible for the subsequent attack on Santa Elena that led to its desertion by the Spaniards.

Spanish relations with Native Americans during the second Santa Elena were certainly not the best. Following its founding in 1577, the emphasis of the leader, Pedro Menéndez Marqués, was on tracking down several hundred Frenchmen who had been given refuge by Indians after surviving a shipwreck at Santa Elena. In this process, Marqués "worked justice before nightfall" on many Frenchmen and burned nineteen Native American villages. History records that at one time Fort San Marcos was attacked by many Indians. In 1587, after the attack on St. Augustine by Sir Francis Drake, Santa Elena was ordered to be abandoned. The houses were burned and fort San Marcos was dismantled, after which thirty-three citizens of Santa Elena filed suit for the loss of their homes.

Stone arrowheads.

With the documented attacks on Forts San Felipe and San Marcos, we expected in our excavations at these forts to find considerable physical evidence of these conflicts in the form of arrowheads. In spite of the fact that hundreds of arrows were shot into Fort San Felipe during the attack in 1576, only two chipped stone arrowheads were recovered. This is likely due to the fact that not all arrows were tipped with stone points.

Stone arrowheads were not an essential feature of Indian warfare. Documents indicate that coastal Indians did not use stone arrowheads, but tipped their arrows with bits of shell, turkey cock spurs, and fish scales. Such arrowheads might not be recognized as such by archaeologists. Even an arrow with only a sharpened wooden tip, when shot through the body, could create a fatal wound. According to the records, many fatal wounds were received by Spaniards from Native American arrows.

Fire arrows shot by Native American bows, and flaming torches thrown onto the palmetto thatched roofs, were effective in destroying the houses in Santa Elena and the *casa fuerte* inside Fort San Felipe. Evidence of this destructive power is seen in the charcoal from burned timbers of the northwest bastion of the fort and in the burned *casa fuerte* posts.

When the Native Americans attacked and killed Moyano and nineteen of his men, they used wooden clubs as well as arrows to accomplish this victory over the Spaniards.

A powerful weapon wielded by the Indians against the few dozen Spaniards inside Fort San Felipe was the psychological impact of the shouts of five hundred Indians storming the fort, against which the arquebus, the sword, the crossbow and the bronze artillery, could not prevail.

Archaeology often does not reveal many things known to have been present in past events, such as the sound of the drumbeats heard during the victory celebration and the dance ceremony following the expulsion of the Spaniards from Santa Elena.

Although we were primarily interested in the Native American things associated with the Spanish occupation period, we also found evidence of Native Americans living on the site for thousands of years. Mixed with other remains from Fort San Felipe, we found fiber tempered and Thom's Creek pottery, dating from about two thousand years before Christ, and Deptford pottery from the time of the Christian era, testimony that Native Americans had long lived there before the Spaniards arrived.

Chapter 16

Plantation Period Discoveries

With the abandonment of the second Santa Elena in 1587, the site returned to its wild state, with occasional visits from Native Americans and Spanish missionaries in the centuries to follow. But we have found no trace of these visits.

The area became a frontier between the Spanish and English. The English plantation economy brought new farmers to the site where Spanish and Native American farmers once lived. They raised cash crops such as indigo and rice and cotton. Our excavations revealed evidence of this period of history on what came to be known as Parris Island.

Tabby walls made of oystershells, and brick footings, are evidence for plantation house ruins of the nineteenth century on the Santa Elena site near Fort San Felipe. In our sifting, a few fragments of seventeenth and early eighteenth century ceramics were found, as were early nineteenth century objects. For two hundred years during the British colonial period, and during the nineteenth century, the plantation way of life was carried out on the island with African slaves providing the labor force where Spaniards had trod. Africans were forcibly brought to live and work, bringing their beliefs with them. The remains they left behind provide fascinating information about this plantation period.

In digging holes for a sample square study of the area north of Fort San Felipe, a total of twelve grave outlines were discovered. These burials were not excavated. Only the grave outlines were plotted just below the topsoil zone.These graves represent only a small percentage of the number that would be found if the area were totally excavated.

On a site about 30 feet from the northwest bastion of Fort San Felipe, a single tombstone stands, on which is engraved,

"William S. Binyard - Born July 6, 1904 - Died Jan. 3, 1909 - Gone but not forgotten." I spoke with Woodrow Garvin, Grounds Superintendent for the Marine Corps Golf Course adjacent to the Santa Elena site about the gravestone, and he stated that a very elderly resident of the black community (one hundred years old) said that the graveyard was known as the "Means Graveyard", and long had been used to bury dead, before the Navy and United States Marine Corps arrived on Parris Island late in the nineteenth century.

In the Mill's Atlas for Beaufort District in 1825, the name "Means" is written on the map where the site of Santa Elena is located. The names in the Mills Atlas usually designate plantation owners' names. Putting together the oral history from the informant with the documented map, I understood that the graveyard I had found was likely for the African slaves working at the Means Plantation, at least as early as 1825, and possibly before then, into the eighteenth century.

The 1909 tombstone of William Binyard marked the only identified grave, but after that, I understand, burials continued to be made there by members of the black community, even after the land was taken over by the United States Government for Marine Corps use when the occupants of the area were dispossessed.

Discovered during the excavation of the northwest bastion of Fort San Felipe were the outlines of two graves from this cemetery. One of these had a nineteenth century period glass tumbler near the top of the grave, with a hardened white chalky substance in the glass, probably medicine. The practice of placing medicine bottles and other objects on graves is related to a black burial practice thought to help keep the spirit of the dead at peace.

When we uncovered the outline of the northwest bastion of Fort San Felipe we found a small charcoal pit, about a foot across, that had been dug into the backfilled soil of the bastion. This pit contained wood charcoal and 3,481 burned glass beads, predominately blue, white, and striped blue-white-and-coral. Later, further south, beneath the eighth fairway of the golf course, two additional burned bead pits were discovered. One of these contained an eighteenth century tobacco pipe stem fragment, helping us to date these bead pits to that period of time.

Because I had found no beads like those from this pit in any Spanish pit or ditch on the site, and since it intruded, or cut into, the filled-in moat of Fort San Felipe, it obviously dated later than the Spanish period of Fort San Felipe. But how much later?

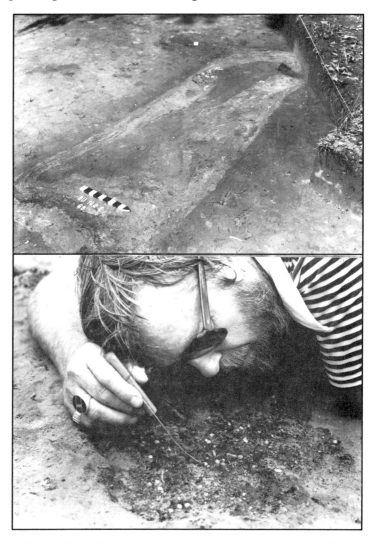

The outline of one of the graves in the Means Graveyard and Stanley South uncovering the beads and charcoal in the pit where over three thousand glass beads had been burned, probably as part of a 19th century funeral.

Bead experts suggested the beads could be from the Spanish period, but I disagreed, because not a single bead of the type in the pits was associated with Spanish artifacts. The seven beads found in Spanish pits were unlike any of those found here. My interpretation was that these mysterious bead pits dated to the eighteenth or early nineteenth century because of the associated pipestem and the absence of such beads in Spanish features. I believe they were connected to some African American ceremony involving the burial of the dead.

The area of Beaufort, South Carolina, the nearest settlement to Parris Island, is a place where African beliefs are still prevalent today and where root men still practice their art. Nearby is the African-modeled Yoruba ceremonial center, Oyotunji, where a series of festivals honoring a pantheon of gods is held throughout the year under the leadership of King Oba Oseijeman Adefumi I, who was very helpful in providing information of voodoo beliefs. I learned from this very erudite man that some African funerals involve two ceremonies, one when the physical body is buried and a second one when material goods are burned so they can accompany the soul to the spirit world.

Beads are a status symbol among Yoruba believers and are among the items burned after the death of an individual. Many Yoruba slaves were brought to South Carolina. It might well be that this practice of burning material possessions is responsible for the burned beads in pits I found. I learned that blue, white, and coral beads are the colors of Olokun, the Yoruba god of the deep sea, similar to Neptune, and that beads of that color were also symbolic of Yemoja, goddess of the Ogun River at Abeokuta, the holy city of Yemoja, and that chiefs or persons of title and royalty wore several strings of such beads. The blue, white, and coral beads I found may well relate to African American beliefs.

Because African Americans lived on and farmed Parris Island for over two hundred years it is not surprising this evidence, in the form of a cemetery and ritual pits filled with thousands of burned blue, white and coral beads, is found. Future archaeology on the nearby plantation sites should reveal far more evidence of the presence on Parris Island of blacks and the plantation owners from the plantation period. Future archaeology at Parris Island is the subject of the next chapter.

Chapter 17

Looking Toward Future Archaeology

Archaeology at Santa Elena has just begun. Only about five percent of Santa Elena and Forts San Felipe and San Marcos has been exposed to reveal the wealth of information not recorded by history. We have not yet discovered the church, nor the cemetery, nor the plaza, nor the town plan, nor a street. Nor have we excavated the interior of Fort San Marcos or the moat of Fort San Felipe. The treasure of information contained by these sites remains to be revealed in future archaeology.

Of the sixty houses known to have been in the second Santa Elena in 1580, one was discovered in the 1991 archaeological season. Only five other building ruins have been found that were probably part of the first Santa Elena. Many more house ruins must be revealed and mapped before we can have a large enough sample to begin to visualize the layout of the two Santa Elenas and their relationship to each other.

Status differences, as seen in the size of the houses and the type of objects associated with them, have only begun to be revealed. Much work needs to be done to enable us to distinguish the dwelling places of the leaders of Santa Elena from the soldiers and those who supplied the energy through labor to keep the town alive. In future archaeology we will continue to be interested in comparing the energy supplied by the wealthy class and the labor force in contrast with other such settlements, such as those established by the English and the French during the sixteenth and seventeeth centuries. For instance, we are interested in the reasons some settlements, such as Jamestown, Virginia, survived, while Santa Elena did not.

We would also like to know more about the roles of the women and children at Santa Elena. We know that when Fort San Felipe was abandoned, there were over three times the number of women and their children than men in the settlement. We will be attempting to learn more about the role of women and their children in Spanish colonial society as reflected by the objects they used in their daily lives, such as ceramics, glassware, clothing and toys.

We will continue to explore the relationship between Native Americans and the Spanish colonists as reflected in the artifacts of each group. Our work so far has clearly revealed the strong interaction between Spaniards and Native Americans through the pottery vessels recovered from Santa Elena and her forts. We also want to learn more about the burned bead pits thought to result from African American burials. This is the kind of information that never will be forthcoming from historical documentation alone.

We have found in our testing that the archaeological record at Fort San Marcos only had been sampled by Major Osterhout's 1923 dig. Much more remains there to be revealed in future projects. Surviving maps of this fort are a valuable adjunct to the archaeological record remaining to be revealed. The comparison of this fort with the maps and the earlier Fort San Felipe will be of major interest when total excavation of Fort San Marcos is carried out.

Future archaeology will, no doubt, present us with additional bonuses from the plantation period like the cremated bead pits. The insights provided by such unexpected discoveries from the plantation period are totally dependent upon archaeology to reveal their existence. We anticipate further clues to this period and the people who left them as archaeology continues.

The 1991 season of excavation and education was sponsored by the Columbian Quincentennial Commission of South Carolina as a major project. Similar projects in 1992 and 1993 are scheduled from funds donated to the Commission by interested individuals and businesses. A major aspect of this sponsorship is an educational experience, wherein school students tour the site while excavations are underway in April and May. Guides explain what the archaeology is revealing as students watch, providing a direct unforgettable experience as to the role archaeology plays in understanding our past.

Tommy Charles taking notes during the 1991 expedition, as Christopher Judge explains archaeology and Santa Elena to one of the many school groups visiting the site during excavation on the Santa Elena site.

The Columbian Quincentennial Commission of South Carolina and the South Carolina Institute of Archaeology and Anthropology are located at 1321 Pendleton Street, Columbia, South Carolina, 29208. Their telephone number is: (803) 777-8172.

Through the sponsorship of the Commission I will return to Santa Elena in April and May of 1992 and 1993. During these field seasons I will again step through the doorway to the past through excavations in Santa Elena to find more buildings in the city and to explore her forts. The site will be open to the public, and school children from across the region will be encouraged to visit the site and learn firsthand about South Carolina's early history that unfolded one hundred years before the coming of the English.

Other published sources of information on Santa Elena, including those I have used in this booklet, are listed in the Reference section. You might want to obtain a copy of Lawrence S. Rowland's recently published (1990) historical story of the events involving Santa Elena, entitled *Window on the Atlantic: the Rise and Fall of Santa Elena, South Carolina's Spanish City,* published by the South Carolina Department of Archives and History. Eugene Lyon's 1984 summary, *Santa Elena: A Brief History of the Colony, 1566-1587,* is available from the South Carolina Institute of Archaeology and Anthropology.

View of the area opened in the 1991 expedition showing pie plates on some of the postholes for the Santa Elena house we discovered. The pie plates on the grass indicate where we think additional postholes for this house will be found in future excavations. The corner posthole had two postmolds in it.

Chapter 18

Out of the Past

As I stood on the site of Spanish Fort San Marcos that first day in 1978, near the monument to French Charlesfort, my companions walked away from the fort to the North carrying the map of Fort San Marcos showing the cannon pointing to Santa Elena and Fort San Felipe. They were looking for a likely spot to dig to search for Santa Elena. A melancholy mood suddenly overcame me. I lingered behind, holding in my hand the Spanish and Indian potsherds and the musketball I had found beneath my feet. They seemed to glow in my hand. I saw them as symbols of Spain's try at establishing a toe-hold on a new continent occupied by Native Americans, and the struggle between them that followed.

I sat against one of Major Osterhout's concrete fort-outline markers and stared at the fuzzy outlines of my companions in the woods to the north. A dense fog floated out of the marsh enveloping them in a gray cloud. The tide flowed into the moat of the fort where Major Osterhout had found many objects from the Spanish and Indian past. It was a romantic and mystical moment. My companions appeared as ghosts, dimly drifting amid the fog. I thought of the exciting scientific adventure lying ahead. I could see myself enjoying the privilege of removing the soil blanket covering the site, opening the doorway to the past to discover more clues such as those I held in my hand. I was captured in a rare moment where the body is experiencing more than the mind can absorb and the feelings had to find a way out of their imprisonment within me.

I took from my pocket a note pad and began writing in an attempt to capture something of that moment in the mist at Santa Elena.

SANTA ELENA

Beneath our dusty feet
Fort San Marcos' ancient soil
Was a precarious Spanish toe-hold
In a new and splendid world.

And over there somewhere,
Beneath that soaring bird,
Stood Charlesfort of France,
And San Felipe, beneath that sand,
Once the pride of Spain
At Port Royal's gateway
To a vast and virgin land.

Our search was not for Spanish gold,
But for clues to lives unknown;
For ancient cedar walls,
For stains of earth
Where holes once were,
For daily living's treasure
In broken sherd of bowl
And lowly refuse bone;
Symbols of a nation's dream,
With Spanish Empire theme.

Then came the clash of arms
Between Americans at home,
Warmed in tribal band,
And aliens in a foreign land.
Bitter war drove invaders
From the homeland shore
In Indian victory sweet...
But the aliens returned.

Then, beneath our feet,
Not rich, nor beautiful,
Nor elegantly refined,
But splendid in simplicity,
An Indian sherd!
And Spanish Majolica,
With a musket ball beside!

Symbols of a way of life,
Of a city burned,
And human strife
Where many died,
Of a toe-hold gone,
Of a conquest tried,
Of a continent lost,
And human pride.

David South and artist Darby Erd exploring the shoreline at Fort San Felipe.

References

Archivo General de Indias - Seville (AGI) The St. Augustine Foundation data base. The St. Augustine Foundation, Inc. at Flagler College. Center for Historic Research. St. Augustine, Florida.

Alexander, Michael (editor)
 1976 *Discovering the New World.* Harper and Row. New York.

Anderson, Ruth Matilda
 1979 *Hispanic Costume, 1480-1530.* Hispanic Society of America. New York.

Angulo, Diego Iñíguez
 1954 *Ars Hispaniae, historia universal del arte Hispánico. Volumen decimosegundo, pintura del siglo XVI.* Editorial Plus-ultra. Madrid.

Cirlot, J. E.
 1962 *A Dictionary of Symbols.* Philosophical Library. New York.

Connor, Jeannette T.
 1925 *Colonial Records of Spanish Florida: Letters and Reports of Governors and Secular Persons,* translated and edited by J.T.C. Vol. 1. *Florida State Historical Society, Publication 5.* Deland.

 1930 *Colonial Records of Spanish Florida: Letters and Reports of Governors and Secular Persons,* translated and edited by J.T.C. Vol. 2. *Florida State Historical Society, Publication 5.* Deland.

Cooper, J. C.
 1978 *An Illustrated Encyclopaedia of Traditional Symbols.* Thames and Hudson. London.

Culin, Stewart
1907 Games of the North American Indians. *Twenty-fourth Annual Report of the Bureau of American Ethnology*, edited by W.H. Holmes. Washington, D.C.

Deagan, Kathleen
1973 *Mestizaje* in colonial St. Augustine. *Ethnohistory* 20 (1):55-65.

1978 The material assemblage of 16th century Spanish Florida. *Historical Archaeology* 12:43-47. The Society for Historical Archaeology.

Spanish St. Augustine: The Archaeology of a Colonial Creole Community. Academic Press. New York.

1985 The archaeology of 16th century St. Augustine. *The Florida Anthropologist* 38 (1):6-33. The Florida Anthropological Society.

De Bry, Theodore
ca.1596 Sodomites savaged by mastiffs. *Discovering the New World* (1976). Edited by Michael Alexander. Harper and Row. New York.

DePratter, Chester B., Charles M. Hudson, and Marvin T. Smith
1983 The route of Juan Pardo's explorations in the interior Southeast, 1566-1568. The *Florida Historical Quarterly*. The Florida Historical Society.

DePratter, Chester B., and Marvin T. Smith
1980 Sixteenth century European trade in the Southeastern United States: evidence from the Juan Pardo expeditions (1566-1568). *Spanish Colonial Frontier Research*, edited by Henry F. Dobyns. Center for Anthropological Studies. Albuquerque.

DePratter, Chester B., and Stanley South
   1990   Charlesfort: The 1989 search project. *Research Manuscript Series 210.* The University of South Carolina, South Carolina Institute of Archaeology and Anthropology. Columbia.

Dilich, Wilhelm
   1640   *Peribologia Oder Bericht.* Für die Reproduktionsgenehmigung danken wir der Bayerischen Staatsbibliothek München.

Dudnick, Elliott E.
   1971   SYMAP user's reference manual for synagraphic computer mapping. Department of Architecture, University of Illinois at Chicago Circle. Chicago.

Ferguson, George
   1958   *Signs and Symbols in Christian Art.* Oxford University Press. New York.

Goggin, John M.

   1960   The Spanish Olive Jar: an introductory study. *Yale University Publications in Anthropology, No. 62.* New Haven.

   1968   Spanish majolica in the New World. *Yale University Publications in Anthropology No. 72.* New Haven.

Hamlyn, Paul
   1970   *Art Treasures in Spain.* The Hamlyn Publishing Group Limited. London and McGraw-Hill Book Company. New York.

Hoffman, Paul
   1978   Sixteenth-century fortification on Parris Island, South Carolina. Manuscript on file at the National Geographic Magazine, Washington.
Judge, Joseph
   1988   The lost century. *The National Geographic Magazine.* March.

Lister, Florence C. and Robert H. Lister
1974   Maiolica in colonial Spanish America. *Historical Archaeology* 8:17-52.

1976a   A descriptive dictionary for 500 years of Spanish-tradition ceramics (13th through 18th centuries). *Historical Archaeology Special Publication No. 1.*

1976b   Italian presence in tin-glazed ceramics of Spanish America. *Historical Archaeology* 10:28-41.

López-Rey, José
1968   *Velázquez' Work and World.* Faber and Faber. London.

Lorant, Stefan (editor)
1946   *The New World: the First Pictures of America.* Duell, Sloan and Pearce. New York.

Lyon, Eugene
1976   *The Enterprise of Florida.* The University Presses of Florida. Gainesville.

1984   Santa Elena: A brief history of the colony, 1566-1587. University of South Carolina, South Carolina Institute of Archaeology and Anthropology, *Research Manuscript Series 193.* Columbia.

Manucy, Albert
1957   Report on relics from 1923 excavation of fortification site on Parris Island, South Carolina. National Park Service. Manuscript on file at the South Carolina Institute of Archaeology and Anthropology, University of South Carolina. Columbia.

1979   Hispanic folk architecture. Manuscript on file at the South Carolina Institute of Archaeology and Anthropology, University of South Carolina. Columbia.

Mills, Robert
    1965   *Mills' Atlas of South Carolina* (1825). Robert Bearce Wilkins and John D. Keels, Jr. Columbia.

New York Times.
    1979   16th-century Spanish fort found at Parris Island. John Noble Wilford. July 13.

Noël Hume, Ivor
    1982   *Martin's Hundred.* Alfred A. Knopf. New York.

Osterhout, George H.
    1923   After three hundred and fifty years-being the story of Charles' Fort, built by Jean Ribault in 1562 on what is now known as Parris Island, South Carolina, *The Marine Corps Gazette,* pp. 98-109. The United States Marine Corps.

Payne-Gallwey, Sir Ralph, Baronet.
    1958   *The Crossbow: Mediaeval and Modern Military and Sporting: Its Construction, History and Management.* Bramwell House. New York.

Post, W. Ellwood
    1974   *Saints, Signs, and Symbols.* Morehouse-Barlow. Wilton, Connecticut.

Ross, Mary
    1925   The Spanish settlement of Santa Elena (Port Royal) in 1578. *Georgia Historical Quarterly IX* (4):352-379. (Essentially a translation of the inspection of Alvaro Flores de Valdes).

Rowland, Lawrence S.
    1990   *Window on the Atlantic: The Rise and Fall of Santa Elena, South Carolina's Spanish City.* South Carolina Department of Archives and History

Salley, Alexander S., Jr.
    1925   The Spanish settlement at Port Royal, 1565-1586. *South Carolina History Magazine* 26:31-40.

Schöbel, Johannes
    1975 *Princely Arms and Armour.* Translated by M. 0. A.
        Stanton. Barrie and Jenkins. London.

Sill, Gertrude Grace
    1975 *A Handbook of Symbols in Christian Art.* Collier
        Books. New York

South, Stanley
    1979 The search for Santa Elena on Parris Island, South
        Carolina. *University of South Carolina, South
        Carolina Institute of Archaeology and Anthropology,
        Research Manuscript Series* 150. Columbia.

    1980 The discovery of Santa Elena. *University of South
        Carolina, Institute of Archaeology and
        Anthropology, Research Manuscript Series* 165.
        Columbia.

    1982 Exploring Santa Elena 1981. *University of South
        Carolina, South Carolina Institute of Archaeology
        and Anthropology, Research Manuscript Series* 184.
        Columbia.

    1983 Revealing Santa Elena 1982. *University of South
        Carolina, South Carolina Institute of Archaeology
        and Anthropology, Research Manuscript Series* 188.
        Columbia.

    1984 Testing archaeological sampling methods at Fort San
        Felipe 1983. *University of South Carolina, South
        Carolina Instititue of Archaeology and
        Anthropology, Research Manuscript Series* 190.
        Columbia.

    1985 Excavation of the *casa fuerte* and wells at Fort San
        Felipe 1984. *University of South Carolina, South
        Carolina Institute of Archaeology and Anthropology,
        Research Manuscript Series* 196. Columbia.

South, Stanley and William B. Hunt
    1986   Discovering Santa Elena west of Fort San Felipe. *University of South Carolina, South Carolina Institute of Archaeology and Anthropology, Research Manuscript Series* 200. Columbia.

South, Stanley and Russell K. Skowronek and Richard E. Johnson
    1988   Spanish artifacts from Santa Elena. *Anthropological Studies* 7. The University of South Carolina, South Carolina Institute of Archaeology and Anthropology. Columbia.

Strauss, Walter L.
    1975   *The German single-leaf woodcut, 1550-1600.* Abaris Books. New York.

Thomas, David Hurst
    1988   *St. Catherines: An Island in Time.* Georgia History and Culture Series, Georgia Endowment for the Humanities. Atlanta.

Trench, Charles Chenevix
    1972   *A history of marksmanship.* Jarrold and Sons Limited. Norwich. Great Britain.

Waddell, Gene
    1980   *Indians of the South Carolina Lowcountry, 1562-1751.* Southern Studies Program. University of South Carolina. Columbia.

Wilford, John Noble
    1979   16th-century Spanish fort found at Parris Island. *New York Times.* July 13.

Glossary

Aglets -   Copper tips on the ends of laces used to fasten clothing together.

Analysis -   The breaking down of data into parts for understanding their meaning.

Archaeological site - The place where people once lived and left cultural remains.

Archaeology -   A method of learning about the past by examining things that have survived.

Arquebus -   A type of musket fired by means of a rope-like fuse touched into a pan of black powder.

Artifact -   A man-made object.

Bandolier bag -   A soldier's purse for holding musketballs.

Bastion -   The raised earth and wood platform for an artillery piece located at each corner of a fort to allow crossfire against those attacking it.

Blockhouse -   A fortified house.

Bordado -   Embroidered decoration of wire and yarn sewn onto clothing of affluent people in the Spanish colonial era.

Casa fuerte -   A fortified house.

Chiefdom -   A Native American network of villages owing allegiance to a central village controlled by a powerful chief.

Cluster -   A concentration of objects in one area as opposed to few in another.

104

Cofitachequi -	A large Native American town near Camden, South Carolina. Many villages paid tribute to the chief of Cofitachequi before and after the arrival of the Spaniards.
Columbia Plain -	A type of majolica defined by John Goggin.
Concejo -	City government.
Crossbow -	A mechanically cocked bow held and fired like a gun.
Data -	The body of clues collected for examination and interpreted by the archaeologist.
Daub -	Clay mixed with grass or Spanish moss and sand, used to form the walls of a building.
Daub processing pit -	A pit used to mix daub for forming walls of a structure. Often filled with refuse after the structure was completed.
Dot-to-dot map -	A game designed to connect numbered dots to produce the outline of some familiar thing.
Escaupiles -	A quilted armored jacket with metal plates providing protection from arrows and bullets.
Ewer -	A spouted pitcher designed to hold wine.
Excavation -	A place where an archaeologist or contractor has dug.
Expedition -	A project designed to excavate an archaeological site.
Exploratory trench -	A trench dug to the depth of the subsoil to reveal features intruding into the subsoil in order to observe the differences in soil color.

Faggot -
A bundle of small sticks tied together to serve as a substitute log in palisade walls and fortifications.

Feature -
A hole dug into the subsoil of a site, such as a pit, a ditch, a well, or an architectural element.

Figa -
The clenched fist symbolic of the hand of God holding the souls of the saved. Thought to have the power to repel bullets and the evil eye.

Fired clay daub -
Burned fragments of daub walls.

Flagging pin -
A wire with a plastic flag attached.

Flotation -
A method of separating light parts of soil from heavier parts by using water to float off seeds, pollen, and other minute animal and plant remains for analysis of past environment.

Garbage -
Discarded plant and animal remains. Food waste. Refuse.

Goat's-foot-lever -
A lever used to cock a crossbow.

Grid -
The layout of an area into squares to allow the archaeologist to recover artifacts in a controlled manner to discover differences in their distribution in order to interpret past behavior.

Hardware cloth -
Woven wire screen.

Historical Archaeology -
The use of the methods of archaeology and history to learn about the global contact and interaction of various people in the past.

History -	A method of learning about the past interpreted from written documents that have survived.
Indian -	A Native American.
Interpretation -	A statement as to the meaning of data similarities and differences.
La Florida -	The mainland of North America, primarily the area of the southeastern coastal states.
Majolica -	Tin-ash glazed pottery.
Maravadí -	A Spanish copper coin of low value.
Midden -	A deposit of trash and garbage archaeologically revealed.
Moat -	A wide defensive ditch dug around a fort, sometimes filled with water.
Olive jar -	A large clay vessel for holding a variety of materials, either wet or dry.
Oystershell mortar -	A mixture of burned oystershell lime, water and sand used to form a plaster coating over wood or daub in Santa Elena after 1580.
Oystershell plaster -	Lime plaster made from burned oystershells forming a surface coating over wood or clay walls and roofs at Santa Elena after 1580.
Palisade -	A wall built in a ditch and formed by setting posts close together in a row.
Parapet -	An earthen wall of a fort.
Partalot -	A bird motif seen on Spanish majolica pottery.
Pike -	A long pole used to move heavy timbers and as a spear-like defensive weapon.

Pike -   A long pole used to move heavy timbers and as a spear-like defensive weapon.

Pit feature -   Evidence of a hole dug in the past now filled with soil of a different color than the surrounding subsoil.

Plantation Period -   In the southern United States, the period of the 18th and 19th centuries during which plantations were developed and operated.

Posthole -   A stain in the earth showing the location of a hole for holding a post.

Posthole pattern -   A group of postholes forming a line or enclosing an area, representing the location of a wall, building or fence.

Postmold -   A stain within a posthole caused by a rotting or burned post.

Potsherd -   A fragment of a broken pot. A sherd, or shard (British).

Power screen -   A motor-driven sifter screen used to separate artifacts from soil.

Processes
of culture -   Broad phenomena such as status differences, evolutionary change, ethnic differences, subsistence strategies, and expenditure of energy.

Profile -   The vertical section of a feature or excavation unit.

Quetzalquoatl -   The feathered serpent god of the Aztecs in Mexico.

Quincentennial -   The 500th anniversary of Columbus's voyage to the western hemisphere.

Random -   Sample holes positioned on a site by use of a
                            table of hole pattern random numbers to
                            allow random collection of artifacts in an area
                            in order to evaluate their distribution.

"Reading the dirt" -   Observing soil colors, textures and layers in
                            the earth to learn about what went on in the
                            past.

Real -   A Spanish silver coin.

Refuse -   Discarded trash and garbage.

Research frame -   An area of a site from which data are
                            systematically collected.

Ruin -   The remains at the place where a structure
                            once stood.

Sampling -   Collecting part of the data potentially
                            available to approximate the whole.

Sampling design -   A plan for sampling data.

Santo Domingo   A Spanish majolica sherd type defined by
Blue on White   John Goggin.
majolica -

Sherd -   A fragment of a broken pot. A potsherd or
                            shard (British).

Site, archaeological -   The place where people once lived and left
                            cultural remains.

Square -   A unit of measure from a grid layout used to
                            obtain a sample of artifacts from an
                            archaeological site.

Stratified systematic unaligned subsurface sampling design - A
                            method used to sample the artifacts on a site
                            to get an idea of where they are concentrated.

Subsoil -	Undisturbed earth lying beneath disturbed layers of soil on a site.
SYMAP -	A computer program known as synagraphic computer mapping, used to project from a sample of data to the entire area sampled.
Synthesis -	The combination of data into a whole for understanding their meaning.
Tabby -	A building material used in the Southeast in the eighteenth and nineteenth centuries sfor constructing walls from lime from burned oystershells mixed with water poured into molds made of boards.
Thatch -	The vegetable material used to cover a structure to protect it from the elements, such as bundles of grass and palmetto leaves.
Topsoil -	The uppermost layer of disturbed soil above the subsoil.
Transit -	A surveying instrument used to map an area of land accurately .
Trash -	Broken fragments of artifacts and discarded material goods.
Tribute -	Goods paid by Native Americans to chiefdoms or to Spaniards.
Wattle and daub -	Woven vines and sticks plastered with clay used to make walls.
Wattling -	Vines and sticks woven into a matting to onto which clay daub is often applied to form wattle and daub walls.
Well point -	A pointed pipe with holes driven into the ground and attached to a pump to allow water to be pumped from the water table.

About the Author

Stanley South is a Research Professor and archaeologist at University of South Carolina's South Carolina Institute of Archaeology and Anthropology in Columbia, where he has conducted archaeological research since 1969. He received an M.A. in anthropology from the University of North Carolina in Chapel Hill. He is a leader in the field of historical archaeology and has authored a widely used text, *Method and Theory in Historical Archaeology*. He has published numerous articles and monographs, including many on Santa Elena.

South is the recipient of the "Distinguished Alumnus" award from Appalachian University, and the "J.C. Harrington Medal" for historical archaeology from The Society for Historical Archaeology. He is the founder of The Conference on Historic Site Archaeology. Recently he has published two volumes of poetry.